# RELAPSE PREVENTION THERAPY

### with
### Chemically Dependent Criminal Offenders

—

A
Guide
for
Counselors,
Therapists, and
Criminal Justice
Professionals

1. ..
2. A
9. A
10. A
11. C
12. E
13. A
14. A
15. D
16. A
17. E
18. A
19. A
20. A
21. D
22. C
23. C
24. A
25. B
26. D
27. C
28. A
29. A
30. D

## PART TWO

# RELAPSE PREVENTION THERAPY

### with
### Chemically Dependent Criminal Offenders

---

### A Guide for Counselors, Therapists, and Criminal Justice Professionals

By Terence T. Gorski

Based on the GORSKI-CENAPS® Model

Herald House/Independence Press
Independence, Missouri

Copyright © 1994
The CENAPS® Corporation
6147 Deltona Blvd.
Spring Hill, FL 34606
Phone: 352/596-8000 (FAX: 352/596-8002

Additional copies may be obtained from the publisher:
Herald House/Independence Press
1001 West Walnut
P.O. Box 390
Independence, MO 64051-0390
Phone: 1-800-767-8181 or 816/521/3015

Printed in the United States of America
ISBN 0-8309-0644-4

# Contents

# Introduction

This book provides comprehensive guidelines for criminal justice system professionals who deal with chemically dependent criminal offenders. It is designed to be used by counselors, therapists, probation and parole officers, and other criminal justice professionals who do coordination or case management with criminal offenders.

Although the material is simple enough to be understood by people with little professional counseling and therapy training, the techniques are based on sound clinical procedures and as a result can improve the effectiveness of interventions provided by psychologists, social workers, and professional counselors. Because of this the concepts in this book provide an excellent foundation for the multidisciplinary team treatment of chemically dependent criminal offenders.

This book describes basic counseling techniques in simple and easy-to-understand language. The goal is to give you practical guidelines for: (1) recognizing both chemical dependency and criminal personality traits in offenders; (2) designing and monitoring effective recovery programs that help offenders to abstain from the use of alcohol, drugs, and criminal behaviors; and (3) implementing relapse prevention and early intervention strategies that can prevent relapse or rapidly intervene and stabilize the offender should relapse occur.

The primary methods described in this book revolve around the CENAPS Model of Recovery and Relapse Prevention. The CENAPS Model integrates the disease model of both chemical dependency and criminal personality disorder with recent advances in cognitive, affective, and behavioral therapy.* The CENAPS Model is based on the belief that in order to recover, offenders must learn how to abstain from alcohol, other drugs, and criminal behaviors.

Cognitive therapy techniques are directed at changing the irrational thoughts that set offenders up to return to the use of alcohol, drugs, and criminal behaviors. Affective techniques deal with the identification and management of feelings and emotions that drive relapse warning signs. Behavioral therapy techniques teach skills to change the self-defeating behaviors that make the offenders' lifestyle so unmanageable that they turn to the use of alcohol, drugs, and criminal behaviors to escape or cope.

Effective treatment for criminal offenders must focus on problems with both alcoholism and drug dependency and criminal personality disorder. These two disorders are closely related, and there is strong evidence that unless both are dealt with simultaneously, the offender will relapse back into both alcohol and drug abuse and criminal behaviors.

To stay away from alcohol, drugs, and criminal behavior will require two different plans. The first plan is a reactive plan that results from trying to avoid the adverse consequences of alcohol and drug use. This is called a "Push Model" of recovery because the client is being pushed away from these adverse consequences. The second plan is proactive and based on doing positive things to make the new lifestyle of recovery pleasant and enjoyable. This is often called the "Pull Model" because it is based on a person being

---

*Cognitive therapy focuses on changing the way a person thinks. Affective therapy focuses on changing the way people manage their feelings and emotions. Behavioral therapy focuses on changing the way people act. Social therapy focuses on changing the way a person relates to other people on the job, at home, and with friends. The first goal is to change from using addictive thoughts, feelings, and behaviors that lead an offender back to chemical use to sobriety-centered behavior that helps them to stay clean and sober. The second goal is to change criminal thoughts, feelings, and behaviors that lead a person back into committing crimes and to replace them with responsible habits of thinking, feeling, and acting.

proactively pulled toward a new way of life that has more rewards and is more satisfying than the old way of life (Helgoe, 1989).

The CENAPS Model uses **Relapse Prevention Therapy (RPT)** to work with the "push" dynamics of recovery. In early recovery most offenders are primarily motivated to deal with the adverse consequences caused by their chemical dependency and criminal personality traits. In other words, they are pushed away from the problems that were created by these disorders. Relapse prevention therapy, which focuses on identifying and managing relapse warning signs, is ideally suited to help offenders develop concrete and specific plans to avoid returning to the use of alcohol, drugs, and criminal behaviors that have created the problems in their lives.

The CENAPS Model also uses a **Developmental Model of Recovery (DMR)** to work with the "pull" dynamics of recovery. This model suggests that recovery can be divided into six developmental stages; specific growth tasks can be developed for each stage. Rather than simply being pushed away from adverse consequence, the DMR encourages offenders to set up concrete goals for personal growth and development that will proactively pull them into higher quality and more effective living by teaching them life skills that work.

## How to Use This Book

This book provides the basic information necessary to help chemically dependent criminal offenders recover and avoid relapse. This book provides a detailed review of all major aspects of recovery and relapse prevention. This background information is important to all members of the treatment team who work with chemically dependent criminal offenders on any level.

I suggest you read the entire book even if some sections do not specifically address the role you play with the criminal offender. The more you understand about the entire recovery process, the better you will be able to fulfill your professional role in the recovery process. By understanding what other team members are doing you will be able to support their role and avoid unnecessary conflicts and confusion.

Chapter 6, "Relapse Prevention Therapy with Criminal Offenders," explains how to use the exercises from *The Relapse Prevention Workbook for the Criminal Offender*. It is helpful to have the workbook available to review the exercise worksheets as you read the description of how the clinical exercises work. It is also important for your training to imagine yourself in the position of a relapse prone offender and complete the exercises in the workbook. This will give you first-hand knowledge of what the offender will experience as he or she works to complete the exercises. It will also help you to understand how the exercises work.

It is important to tell the offenders you are working with that they may get discouraged at times when they are completing the workbook. The main reason for this is that chemically dependent people, especially criminal offenders, want immediate payoffs and results. Recovery doesn't give immediate results. Encourage them to continue and give them positive feedback for each step they accomplish along the way.

It is also important for *you* not to get discouraged. Talk with other people who are doing the same kind of work. Find out what is working and what is not working for them. Peer support and encouragement is necessary to keep from burning out.

How do you know when a patient is making progress? You will know by seeing how the patients change the way they think, feel, and act toward themselves and those around them.

If you try to control your patients, they will either drop out of treatment or simply tell you what they think you want to hear.

You must view your patients as people whose chemical dependency and criminal personality traits prevent them from acting in a socially acceptable manner. These patients want to be full members of society, but they do not have the skills and in some cases have given up hope.

Recognize that it is your job to help recovering offenders understand more about themselves and their chemical dependency and criminal personality traits. It is your job to work collaboratively with them to learn new skills and help them to have hope so that they are motivated to change.

You may not have all the answers, but you can listen and try to understand what the recovering offender is trying to tell you. You can guide him or her through a series of exercises and discuss the thoughts and feelings that the offender experiences as a result. You can work together to find the key to recovery and relapse prevention. This professional guide and its companion relapse prevention workbook will give you a broad foundation of skills to allow this to happen.

It is important to learn from recovering offenders that you work with. Not all will recover, but those who relapse can teach you important information that can help others to recover. If you can learn from all of your experiences, positive and negative, you will become a better counselor. Remember that your best source of information is your patients. When you make a mistake, admit it, and learn from it.

Now it is time to roll up your sleeves and start learning the basics about chemical dependency, criminal personality traits, the recovery process, the relapse process, and relapse prevention therapy.

# Chapter 1

# Chemical Dependency
## A Biopsychosocial Model

Chemically dependent criminal offenders generally suffer from two disorders: *chemical dependency*, which makes them unable to control their alcohol and drug use, and *criminal personality traits*, which make it difficult for them to regulate their behavior and conform with the rules set down by legitimate authority.

Chemical dependency and criminal personality traits must be treated together because they are closely related. Chemical dependency often pushes a person into criminal behavior. At times the loss of impulse control that occurs during intoxication causes people to make poor judgments and do things they normally would not do. At other times they consciously plan and execute crimes to support their addiction. Many chemically dependent criminal offenders, however, have antisocial personality traits that caused them to commit crimes before they began to use, abuse, or became addicted to drugs.

People with criminal personality traits are driven to commit crimes—and often enjoy doing so. Their criminal personality often pushes them to abuse alcohol and drugs in order to get the courage to commit crimes or to deal with the stress of avoiding capture after the crime is committed. Many get caught because alcohol and drug use impaired their thinking and behavior; they got sloppy and careless, making mistakes that resulted in their arrest.

*Chemical dependency and criminal personality traits must be treated together.*

One of the critical roles that needs to be played by criminal justice system professionals is that of educator. We must teach criminal offenders about what is wrong with them and what they need to do to recover from both chemical dependency and criminal personality traits. With exposure to accurate information, access to recovery resources, and continued support and rapid intervention if treatment recommendations are violated, many chemically dependent criminal offenders can and do recover.

This chapter will present the basic information that professionals and recovering criminal offenders need to know about chemical dependency. The next chapter will present the information about criminal personality.

## Mood-altering Chemicals (MACs)

In order to talk about chemical dependency we have to define some terms. The term chemical refers to mood-altering or mind-altering drugs. These drugs have the power to change how we think, feel, and act by changing the way our brain works. There are four basic types of mood-altering chemicals (MACs): uppers, downers, mind benders, and pain killers.

**Mood-altering Chemicals (MACs)**
1. Uppers—Stimulants
2. Downers—Sedatives and sleeping pills
3. Mind Benders—Perception distorters
4. Pain Killers—Sensation blockers / Narcotics

**Uppers** are the stimulant drugs such as cocaine and amphetamines that stimulate or charge up the brain. People like to use stimulants because they speed them up and make them feel strong, energetic, and powerful.

Downers are sedatives such as alcohol, Librium, Valium, barbiturates, and other sleeping pills that slow the brain down and make people feel calm or relaxed.

Please notice that alcohol is included in this list. *Alcohol is a drug!* It is the most commonly used drug in the United States, and more people are injured as a result of its use and abuse than as a result of all other drugs combined. People like to use downers (including alcohol) to calm themselves down, relax, and get to sleep. Many people who are addicted to uppers will use downers to deal with the excessive speeding and crashes that accompany addiction to uppers.

**Mind benders** are perception-distorting drugs such as LSD, PCP, hashish, and marijuana that change the way we see ourselves, others, and the world. People use mind benders to intensify spiritual experiences, to try to find new ways of experiencing life, or simply to experience new and different things. They seek altered states of consciousness and use mind-bending drugs as a way to do that.

**Pain killers** are narcotics, such as heroine and morphine, that block out pain and produce a deep state of euphoria. People like to use pain killers to escape from unpleasant realities and make the world go away for a little while.

15

# How Common Is Alcohol and Other Drug Use?

The use of alcohol and other drugs is very common. About two-thirds (66 percent) of adults in the United States drink alcohol. One-third abstain totally or drink so infrequently that for all practical purposes they abstain.

About one-third (34 percent) of all adults are light drinkers who drink less than twice per month and rarely if ever get drunk. These light drinkers consume less than 10 percent of all the alcohol sold.

About one-fourth (24 percent) of all adults are moderate drinkers who drink two to three times per week and, when they do drink, they rarely have more than two to three drinks. These moderate drinkers consume about one-fourth (26.3 percent) of all the alcoholic beverages sold.

About 10 percent of the adult population are heavy drinkers who drink daily, often to the point of intoxication. This 10 percent of the population consumes 66 percent of all alcoholic beverages sold. It is estimated that 10 percent of the adult population suffer from alcoholism and that most drinking alcoholics fall into the category of heavy drinkers.

Drug use is also common among adults. Many adults have experimented with mood-altering drugs other than alcohol, and at least 5 percent of the population has serious problems with drug abuse or addiction.

This means that about 15 percent of all adults have problems with alcohol and drug abuse. The average person has a greater than one-in-ten chance of becoming addicted at some time during his or her life. If you are a criminal offender, the odds are even greater that you will have an alcohol or drug abuse problem.

## Alcohol, Drugs, and Criminality

Nearly all criminals have experimented with alcohol and other drugs, and the vast majority use alcohol and drugs regularly and heavily whenever they can. It is estimated that 70 percent of all criminal offenders have serious problems with alcohol and other drugs and that their use of alcohol and drugs has in some ways caused or complicated their legal problems.

About 48 percent of all criminals, for example, were under the influence of alcohol at the time they committed their crimes. Look at these statistics for people convicted of different crimes: 54 percent of people convicted of violent crimes were drunk at the time of the crime; 40 percent of those convicted of property crimes; 29 percent of those convicted of drug crimes; and 54 percent of those committing public order crimes.

Crime is rarely a symptom of the nonaddictive use of illegal drugs in people who do not have chemical-use disorders or criminal-personality disorders. Fewer than 5 percent of all criminal offenders would fall into this category. Most criminal offenders who commit alcohol and drug-related crimes (approximately 80 percent) have serious chemical-use disorders. About 15 percent commit crimes to support their addiction; the other 65 percent are chemically dependent and also have a criminal personality disorder that contributes to their history of criminality.

The conclusion is that most criminal offenders use, abuse, or become addicted to alcohol and other mood-altering drugs. Their drug abuse and addiction contribute in significant ways to their criminal behavior and, unless the chemical dependency is identified and treated, these offenders are at high risk of relapse. This is demonstrated by the fact that most repeat criminals have alcohol and drug problems. Alcohol and drug use among parolees are associated with breaking parole and probation, renewed criminal behavior, and new arrests and convictions. Few criminal offenders are social drinkers or recreational drug users.

## Defining Chemical Dependency

Chemical dependency is a broad term used to describe people who have problems as a result of alcohol and drug use. To describe what this means, let's separate all people who use alcohol and drugs into two categories: (1) those who use alcohol and drugs and never have any problems as a result of their use—we will call these people *social drinkers* and *recreational drug users*; and (2) those who have problems as a result of their use of alcohol and drugs—we will say that these people have a *chemical-use disorder*. The two terms, chemical-use disorder and chemical dependency, can be used as equivalent or interchangeable terms for the purpose of this discussion.

## Chemical-use Disorders

People with chemical-use disorders use alcohol and drugs in a way that causes physical, psychological, and social problems. As a general rule, any person who has problems as a result of chemical use and continues to use in spite of the problems probably has a chemical-use disorder.

People with chemical-use disorders use alcohol regularly and heavily. **Regular use** means that they have a habit of drinking frequently and at certain predictable intervals. For example, many people with chemical-use disorders are daily drinkers, while others drink heavily on weekends but abstain during the week. **Heavy use** refers to how much alcohol or drugs are consumed during a typical episode of use. The more consumed, the heavier the use. Two questions can be used to determine how regularly and heavily someone uses alcohol and drugs: (1) How much do you use? and (2) How often do you use it?

Regular and heavy use can result in psychosocial dependence. The term *psychosocial* is a combination of two words—"psycho" meaning psychological and "social" meaning relationships with people. People are said to be psychologically dependent when they rely on alcohol and drugs to help manage their thoughts, feelings, or behaviors. A person is socially dependent when he or she needs to drink or use drugs to deal with, get along with, or enjoy becoming involved with other people.

*Any person who has problems as a result of alcohol or drug use and continues to use in spite of the problems probably has a chemical-use disorder.*

People can depend on alcohol and drugs to help them do things that they are unable to do without it (such as relax, feel confident around other people, or have a good time) or to stop doing things that they feel they must do when sober (such as stay home with the spouse and kids all the time). Because most people with chemical-use disorders rely on alcohol and drugs to change something about who they are and what they do, most have a dual personality. They act one way when they are sober and another way when they have been drinking and drugging.

In evaluating someone's alcohol and drug-use pattern, there are two helpful questions: (1) What does alcohol allow you to do or be that you can't do or be without it? and (2) What do alcohol and drugs allow you to stop doing or being that you feel you must do when you are sober?

People with chemical-use disorders develop problems as a result of their use. These problems can be personal, social, or occupational. **Personal problems** result in subjective feelings of pain or discomfort that don't affect other people. These personal problems include shame, guilt, remorse, and low self-esteem. **Social problems** involve conflicts that develop between chemically dependent people and other people in their lives. This typically involves problems with family, friends, and associates. **Occupational problems** involve difficulties at work and include such things as tardiness, absenteeism, accidents, problems with supervisors and coworkers, and inconsistent job performance.

To summarize, people with chemical-use disorders (1) use alcohol regularly and heavily, (2) become dependent on alcohol to function psychologically and socially, and (3) develop social and occupational problems as a result of their use.

## Types of Chemical-use Disorders

There are two different types of chemical-use disorders: abuse disorders and dependence disorders.

People with **abuse disorders** depend on and get into trouble with alcohol and drugs but do not become physically dependent. People with **dependence disorders** get into trouble with alcohol and drugs and also become physically dependent. The signs of this physical dependence are tolerance, withdrawal, and illness.

20

Tolerance is the ability to consume large amounts of alcohol and drugs without acting or feeling intoxicated. Because chemically dependent persons can use large amounts with no apparent adverse affects, they drink and drug heavily enough to become physically dependent. Physical dependence is marked by the development of physical withdrawal symptoms when the person attempts to stop using.

---

### Chemical-use Disorders

*Abuse Disorders*
- Psychosocial Dependence
- Problems from Use
- No Physical Dependence

*Can lead to*

*Dependence Disorder*
- Abuse Disorder
- Physical Dependence (tolerance, withdrawal)
- Physical Illness

---

Alcohol and other drugs can damage a variety of organ systems in the body. When people develop physical damage related to the chronic use of alcohol and other drugs, it is almost certain that they have become physically dependent.

## Abuse Disorders

Chemical abuse results from the use of mood-altering chemicals by people who are psychosocially predisposed to become dependent. **Psychological predisposition** to alcohol and drug abuse occurs in people who grow up in families that teach them that it is okay to use alcohol and drugs to manage your feelings and behaviors and that people should not be held responsible for what they do under the influence of alcohol and other drugs. Social predisposition occurs when people are taught as children that it is normal and natural to drink regularly, heavily, and abusively and to use alcohol and drugs as the primary way to have fun and to deal with other people.

When people define regular, heavy, and problematic drinking as normal, dependency is just a swallow away. Because dependence upon alcohol and drugs is viewed as normal and natural, they are less likely to recognize that they have a problem until severe problems develop and persist for a long period of time. This lack of recognition is called **denial**. When people are in denial, they find it difficult to recover because they don't believe they have problems with alcohol and drugs and, as a result, are unwilling to try and stop using. Chemical use in psychosocially predisposed people can lead to psychosocial dependence, personal distress, social and occupational problems, and denial that any of these problems exist.

## Dependence Disorders

Chemical dependency results from chemical use in genetically predisposed people. There are four genetically influenced traits that increase the likelihood that someone will become alcohol or drug dependent: biological reinforcement, high tolerance, hangover resistance, and brain damage sensitivity.

People with **biological reinforcement** feel really good when they use alcohol and other drugs. They experience positive mood and personality changes when they are using, and as a result they want to use more. Many researchers believe that chemically dependent people are born with deficiencies in certain chemicals in their brains and, when they use their drug of choice, these brain chemicals normalize and they feel normal and fully functional. When they stop using their drug of choice, these brain chemicals become imbalanced again and they feel uncomfortable and irritable and have difficulty thinking and functioning normally.

People with **high tolerance** are able to consume large amounts of alcohol or drugs without feeling or looking intoxicated. As a result, they believe they can handle alcohol or drugs well and are immune from any adverse effects of heavy use. People with **hangover resistance** are capable of drinking and drugging very heavily the night before and experience mild or no hangovers the next morning.

How much of this is a natural occurrence as compared to consequence of abuse?

---

**Genetically Influenced Tendencies**

*Biological Reinforcement*
- Positive mood and personality change

*High Tolerance*
- Heavy use without intoxication

*Hangover Resistance*
- Minimal illness the day after use

*Brain Damage Sensitivity*
- Brain dysfunction buildup with regular use

---

As you look at these three genetically inherited tendencies—biological reinforcement, high tolerance, and hangover resistance—it is easy to understand why genetically predisposed people continue to use alcohol and drugs. The biological reinforcement causes them to feel really good when they drink and use drugs. Alcohol and drugs actually become a psychoactive medicine that improves their mood and personality. They can drink large amounts without getting drunk because of their high tolerance. They rarely, if ever, get sick or hung over the next day. They say to themselves, "Since using alcohol and drugs feels so good, and I can use a lot without getting intoxicated and I feel fine the next morning, why not keep using?"

The answer to this question is simple and can be summarized in three words: **brain damage sensitivity**. People who are genetically predisposed to become chemically dependent

23

will suffer more severe brain damage when using the same amount of alcohol and drugs as other people. If two people who are the identical height and weight were to drink the same amount of alcohol over the same period of time, you would expect that they would have the same consequences. Unfortunately, this is not true. If one person (Person "A") is genetically predisposed to become alcoholic and the other person (Person "B") is not, A would experience more brain damage than B even though they drank the same amount over the same period of time. Even worse, it would take A's brain far longer to return to normal than B's.

So here is the problem: people who are genetically predisposed to chemical dependency feel better when using alcohol and drugs, can use larger amounts without becoming intoxicated, and rarely get hangovers. Unfortunately, they are damaging their brain and rapidly progressing in the disease of chemical dependency. The problem is they don't know it. It's like shooting athletes full of Novocain to perform despite an injury. They can cripple themselves up and never feel any pain.

## Chemical Dependency as a Biopsychosocial Disease

Chemical dependency is a biopsychosocial disease. "Bio" means biological or of the body. "Psycho" means psychological or of the mind. Social means pertaining to relationships and societal obligations. The *biological* aspects of chemical dependency involve brain dysfunction caused by chemical use in genetically predisposed people. The *psychological* aspects of chemical dependency involve personality change that is caused by the brain dysfunction resulting from chronic alcohol and drug poisoning. The *social* aspects of chemical dependency consist of lifestyle problems caused by the personality change.

24

**Chemical Dependency Is a Biopsychosocial Disease**
*Bio = Biological (of the body)*
- *Brain dysfunction caused by addictive use in genetically predisposed people*

*Psycho = Psychological (of the mind)*
- Personality change caused by brain dysfunction

*Social = Relationships (of society)*
- Lifestyle problems caused by the personality changes

Look at the progression of problems. When genetically predisposed people use alcohol and drugs, they suffer brain damage. As the brain damage slowly progresses, they develop personality problems because their ability to think clearly, manage their feelings and emotions, and self-regulate their behavior becomes impaired. These personality changes cause problems in their relationships at home, with friends, and on the job. Another way to say this is that chemical use in genetically predisposed people causes brain dysfunction, personality change, and social and occupational impairments.

## The Progression of Chemical Dependency

Chemical dependency is a progressive disease that moves through four predictable stages: a prodromal stage, an early stage, a middle stage, and a chronic stage. The **Prodromal Stage** is marked by regular and heavy use in someone with either psychosocial predisposition, genetic predisposition, or both. The **Early Stage** is marked by a growing dependence on alcohol and other drugs. People begin to need alcohol and other drugs to function normally. When they try to stop using, they don't feel right and develop problems. When they start drinking and drugging again, things seem to go back to normal.

*4 Stage of Chemical Depending*

25

*1. Prodromal - regular use by someone w/ predisposition*
*2. Early - growing dependence*
*3. Middle - progressive loss of control*
*4. Chronic - marked neuropsychological deterioration*

The **Middle Stage** is marked by a progressive loss of control. This loss of control usually begins when people can't stop drinking or drugging when they planned. They stay out later, use more, and spend more money than they intended. Next, they start losing control over what they do while using. They may go into blackouts or do things they normally would not do. Finally, they lose control over their ability to abstain. They can't stay clean and sober, no matter how hard they try. The longer they are sober the worse they feel. These bad feelings cause obsession (out-of-control thinking about alcohol and drug use), compulsion (the irrational urge to use alcohol and drugs despite knowing its adverse consequences), and craving (a body or tissue hunger for alcohol and drugs that makes them physically uncomfortable and desire greater alcohol or drug use than they wanted originally).

---

### The Progression of Chemical Dependency
*Prodromal Stage*
- Regular and heavy alcohol/drug use

*Early Stage*
- Growing dependency

*Middle Stage*
- Progressive loss of control

*Chronic Stage*
- Biopsychosocial deterioration

---

The **Chronic Stage** is marked by physical, psychological, and social deterioration. The person gets physically sick from the excessive use of alcohol and drugs and starts developing obvious mental and emotional problems. He or she can't think clearly, manage feelings and emotions, or control behaviors. As a result, serious social problems develop. Marriages become strained. Separation and divorces are common. Sober friends are replaced by drinking and drugging buddies. Job problems develop, eventually leading to termination and unemployment.

*Chemical dependency is a progressive disease.* This means that once people begin experiencing the early stage symptoms, they are very likely to experience progressively more severe problems unless they stop all alcohol and drug use and seek treatment to help them to stay sober and make the personality and lifestyle changes needed to find a meaningful and comfortable life in sobriety.

## Personality and Chemical Dependency

Many people mistakenly believe chemical dependency is caused by personality problems that developed in childhood. This is not true. If someone believes that chemical dependency is caused by an underlying personality problem, they ignore the drinking and drugging and try to treat the underlying personality problem that caused it. This approach has historically failed and tends to produce relapse rates as high as 98 percent. Research shows that effective treatment for chemical dependency focuses on teaching chemically dependent people how to stop using alcohol and drugs and how to stay stopped.

Personality, however, does play a big role in recovery. To understand why, let's look at the role personality plays in chemical dependency. To do this we need to define two terms: the preaddictive personality and the addictive personality. The **Preaddictive Personality** is the childhood personality that was present before the person began to use alcohol or other drugs. This preaddictive personality is formed as the result of a complex interaction between genetically inherited traits and early childhood experiences.

Any woman who has had more than one child will recognize personality traits even before the child is born. Some children are more active than others. They kick and move

*[handwritten margin note:]* Then, when were the beliefs that produced psychological predisposition) if not in childhood — the formative years?

*[handwritten margin note:]* Makes it sound as if some children are programmed for addictive personality!

27

around a lot. Others are more passive. They hardly move at all. Traits such as energy level, intelligence, and emotional sensitivity are genetically influenced. Once the child is born, he or she is powerfully affected by early childhood environment. The genetically inherited traits interact with how the parents treat them, and the result is the preaddictive personality.

The **Addictive Personality** develops as a result of personality changes caused by the addiction itself. Remember, chemical use in a genetically predisposed person causes brain dysfunction and personality disorganization. In other words, the progressive brain dysfunction that results from chemical use disorganizes the preaddictive personality and creates a secondary addictive personality.

---

### Personality and Chemical Dependency
*Preaddictive Personality*
- Childhood personality present before
  alcohol/drug use began

*Addictive Personality*
- Personality changes caused by the addiction

---

When chemically dependent people get clean and sober by working a recovery program, these addictive personality traits rapidly disappear and the preaddictive personality will emerge once again. If the chemically dependent person was raised in a healthy functional family, a healthy and functional personality will reemerge and the individual will generally recover without relapse. If they were raised in a dysfunctional family, however, the emerging preaddictive personality may be as dysfunctional as the addictive personality. Here's why.

Functional families teach people how to think clearly, logically, and rationally, manage feelings and emotions, behave responsibly, and develop effective work relationships and loving and caring intimate relationships. If the chemically dependent person was raised in a functional family, these kinds of healthy preaddictive personality traits will come back as the symptoms of the addictive personality disappear with recovery. Unfortunately, at least 65 percent of chemically dependent people and nearly 100 percent of criminal offenders were raised in dysfunctional families.

Dysfunctional families fail to teach children the basic skills of responsible or effective living. There is often physical or sexual abuse or severe social neglect. The children don't learn basic reasoning and problem-solving skills. They don't learn how to recognize and responsibly manage their feelings and emotions. They don't learn how to self-regulate and take responsibility for their own behavior. Many times their parents suffered from alcoholism, drug dependence, mental illness, or a combination of the three.

As a result, when a chemically dependent person from a dysfunctional family enters recovery, the addictive personality goes into remission and the very self-defeating or dysfunctional preaddictive personality begins to emerge. These people have a dual diagnosis. They are suffering from both chemical dependency and a personality disorder. Many also have other mental disorders such as depression, anxiety and panic attacks, and post traumatic stress disorder. These patients tend to be relapse prone and require proper diagnosis and treatment for all of these problems.

## The Addictive Personality

The addictive personality develops as a result of the progression of chemical dependency and has six common characteristics: obsession, compulsion, loss of behavioral control, personality change, secondary life problems, and denial of addiction.

**Obsession** is out-of-control thinking about alcohol and drug use. The person develops a pattern of irrational thinking called *addictive thinking*. The sole purpose of addictive thinking is to protect the right to use alcohol and other drugs despite evidence that it is not safe to do so. Addictive thinking patterns include denial, rationalization, minimizing, and blaming. These addictive thoughts are used so frequently that they automatically pop into a person's head. Many chemically dependent people are not aware of what addictive thinking is, so these addictive thoughts end up running their lives.

Compulsion is the irrational urge to use alcohol and drugs despite adverse consequences. Many chemically dependent people are confused because in their head they know that alcohol and drug use is dangerous and they want to stop using. Something inside of them, however, drives them to drink even though they don't want to. This is the nature of compulsion. It is an urge that defies rational thought. When compulsion is caused by a tissue hunger or physical need for the drug, it is often called craving. In this book, we will use the term "compulsion to use" and craving interchangeably.

---

### Addictive Personality Characteristics

*Obsession*
- Out-of-control thinking about alcohol/drug use

*Compulsion*
- Irrational urge to use despite adverse consequences

*Loss of Behavioral Control*
- Inability to predict behavior while using

*Personality Change*
- Altered values, attitudes, and beliefs
- Lifestyle problems caused by use

*Denial of Addiction*
- Alcohol/drug use blamed on life problems

---

Loss of behavioral control is the inability to predict behavior while using alcohol and drugs. It occurs when the obsession and compulsion become so strong that people cannot resist them. Loss of control can occur during the use of alcohol and drugs and during periods of abstinence. They find that they can't stay sober because the obsession and compulsion to use is so strong. Once they start, they get into trouble. They often use more alcohol or drugs than they intended. They are unable to stop drinking and drugging when they choose to. They can't control their impulses and often do things while drinking and drugging that they would not have done when sober. Sometimes they black out and cannot remember what they have done.

**Personality change** is a fundamental change in how people view themselves, other people, and the world. In essence, chemically dependent people change as a result of their addiction. Their values are distorted. Alcohol and drug use become more important than anything else. Their attitudes change. They become negative, hostile, and judgmental. Their self-concept swings between grandiosity ("I'm better than everyone else!") to insecurity and low self-worth ("I am worse than everyone else. I am a nothing and everyone knows it, but there is nothing that I can do about it!"). Chemically dependent people often violate their own value system by doing things they know are wrong or by doing things they would not have done sober. This results in constantly feeling ashamed ("I am a defective person who has no worth") and guilty ("I am doing something wrong or am unable to do the right things I need to").

**Secondary life problems** start to develop and become more severe. Problems with friends and family come first. The person starts hanging out with others who abuse and are addicted to alcohol and drugs. His or her life becomes alcohol and drug centered, and sober and responsible people are driven out. Job and money problems develop. Eventually the person loses his or her job and has no money.

31

The most baffling trait of the addictive personality is **denial of addiction**. Despite all these problems, the person believes that he or she is a social drinker and recreational drug user. Such people are unable to identify the relationship between alcohol and drug use and their other life problems. They sincerely believe that they are drinking and using drugs to cope effectively with these problems. They don't believe that alcohol and drug use has caused the problems.

## The Progression to Chemical Dependency

Genetically predisposed people who use and abuse alcohol and other mood-altering chemicals become addicted. Alcohol and drug abuse can progress to chemical dependency. This progression can be described as a continuum of alcohol and drug problems ranging from mild to moderate to severe. Mild problems can be defined as abuse disorders. Severe problems are defined as dependence disorders. It is often difficult to draw the line between the two. Exactly when does abuse (alcohol and drug problems in the absence of physical dependence) become addiction (alcohol and drug problems plus physical dependence)? This is a difficult question to answer, and for all practical purposes it is irrelevant. The fundamental treatment principles for abuse disorders are nearly identical to those for dependence disorders. As a result, we will use the term chemical dependency to describe both abuse disorders and dependence disorders.

## Basic Treatment Principles

Recovery from chemical dependency requires four basic things: (1) abstaining from alcohol and drug use; (2) identifying and changing addictive thoughts, feelings and behaviors; (3) identifying and changing addiction centered lifestyle patterns; and (4) deep personality and value change.

*Continuum of Chemical Dependency*

*Mild problems* . . . . . . . . . . . *Severe problems*

↓ ↓

*Abuse disorders* *Dependence disorders*

32

**Recovery from Chemical Dependency Requires:**
- Abstinence
- Changing addictive thoughts, feelings, and behaviors
- Changing addiction-centered lifestyle patterns
- Deep personality and value change

To recover, chemically dependent people must *abstain from alcohol and drug use*. This means making a commitment not to use alcohol and drugs no matter what happens. This is essential. There is strong evidence that once a person has developed a significant physical or psychological dependence on alcohol or other mood-altering drugs, therapies that teach controlled drinking simply don't work.

To recover, chemically dependent people must also *identify and change addictive thoughts, feelings, and behaviors*. Addictive thoughts, feelings, and behaviors are those that support the use of alcohol and other drugs. Many chemically dependent people stop drinking and drugging but refuse to change anything else. They aren't drinking and drugging, but they keep thinking, feeling, and acting like a drunk and a drug addict. This is often called being in a dry drunk.

Recovery also means *identifying and changing addiction-centered lifestyle patterns*. Chemically dependent people put alcohol and drugs in the center of their lives and expect everything else to revolve around their habits of use. They get jobs that won't interfere with their drinking and drugging. They find partners, lovers, and friends who either drink and drug more than they do or who will support their continued use. For them to get sober, these alcohol and drug-centered lifestyle patterns must be broken. In AA there is a saying, "*If you don't want to slip, don't hang around slippery people, places, and things.*" Chemically dependent people must take the alcohol and drug-centered activities out of their lives and replace them with sobriety-centered activities.

To stay sober requires *deep personality and value change*. It is not enough to change on the outside. Recovery requires change from the inside out. Many chemically dependent people will comply with treatment requirements and temporarily change their lives. But deep inside they are planning their next drink and secretly keeping their drug connections alive. They aren't drinking or using drugs because they are afraid of the consequences. Deep inside, however, their addictive value system has remained unchanged. They still believe that to have the good life, they must use alcohol and drugs, and they feel deprived because the treatment system they have been mandated won't allow them to do that. People must want sobriety. They must want to change.

It is important to remember, however, that this deep personality change requires time. Most chemically dependent people don't want to get clean and sober when they enter treatment. They are forced there by circumstances. Think about it. When is the last time you were walking down the street on a sunny day feeling fine and said to yourself, "Gee, I think I'll go and have a tooth pulled today!" Most people go to the dentist because their teeth hurt or because they know that if they don't go, eventually their teeth will start hurting. The same is true for chemically dependent people. They come into treatment because the circumstances force them to. But this doesn't mean they can't get well. Mandated clients often have higher long-term recovery rates than voluntary clients. This is because when the going gets rough and they want to drop out of treatment, they can't. They have to stay in treatment and work through the tough issues that will allow them to have meaningful and comfortable lives of sobriety. Father Joseph Martin, a priest devoted to helping alcoholics, said it better than I ever could when he said, "You can lead a horse to water, but you can't make him drink—but you sure can hold him there long enough to make him thirsty."

Chemically dependent people are difficult to treat, but they are not impossible to treat. With proper treatment, as many as two-thirds of chemically dependent people can and do recover.

Rethinking alcoholism —

Keeping the program
- replacing negative
pathological view
and labels with
focus on understanding
the positive intentions
of persons who abuse
chemicals to meet
universal needs for
Safety?

belonging?

self-esteem?

love?

power?

purpose?

Why important? — Teach esteem for self
~~Because~~ ~~Build self esteem of~~
~~person~~

Teach practitioners to retain
unconditional regard to protect
themselves from harsh, neg views
of others.

## Chapter 2

# Criminal Personality
## A Biopsychosocial Model

Antisocial behaviors are common among criminal offenders. In the general population about 4 percent of males and 1 percent of females would be diagnosed as having an antisocial personality disorder. Certain groups of people, however, are at higher risks than others. For example, about 15 percent of alcoholic males and 5 percent of alcoholic females have antisocial personality disorders. This is more than four times the incidence in the general population. The incidence of antisocial personality is about 32 percent in male narcotics addicts (eight times that of the general population) and 50-80 percent among prison inmates (Forrest, 1993).

| Incidence of Antisocial Personality Disorder | |
| --- | --- |
| All Males | 4% |
| All Females | 1% |
| Alcoholic Males | 15% |
| Alcoholic Females | 10% |
| Male Narcotics Addicts | 32% |
| Prison Inmates | 50-80% |

37

Among chemically dependent criminal offenders about 65 percent have both criminal personality disorders and chemical dependency. Criminal personality disorder is related to criminal recidivism as evidenced by the fact that most repeat criminals have criminal personality disorders and that criminal personality is often associated with breaking parole and probation, renewed criminal behavior, and new arrests and convictions. Alcohol and drug abuse is often a feature of antisocial personality, so most offenders with criminal personalities also suffer from chemical dependency.

The conclusion is that most habitual criminals have criminal personality disorders or serious criminal personality traits that, in many cases, are complicated by chemical dependency. These offenders need treatment. Few criminal offenders have healthy and functional personalities.

Punishment alone will not stop criminals with criminal personality traits from committing antisocial acts. Treatment alternatives to punishment are needed in order to reduce recidivism rates.

To develop effective treatment alternatives four things are required. First, we must define criminal personality as a biopsychosocial condition so that we can understand how it works and provide appropriate treatment interventions. Second, we must understand the relationship of personality disorders to both criminal behaviors and alcohol and drug use. Criminal personality can cause both and, as a result, any effort to reduce criminal recidivism must be accompanied by the treatment of both criminal personality and chemical dependency.

Third, to treat these disorders we must have clear diagnostic criteria for use in differential diagnosis. We must be able to rapidly discover which offenders have criminal personality traits, chemical dependency, or a combination of the two and then provide appropriate treatment. Finally, we must develop long-term guidelines for treatment that are compatible with the criminal justice system. Treatment alternatives must be integrated into criminal justice procedures at all levels and become an integral part of the system rather than an appendage or add-on program.

*Punishment alone will not stop criminals with criminal personality traits from committing antisocial acts. Treatment alternatives to punishment are needed in order to reduce recidivism rates.*

## What Is Antisocial Behavior?

Antisocial behaviors are any actions that irresponsibly defy established laws, morality, or a sense of justice and fair play. People who use antisocial behaviors refuse to play by the rules or follow the leadership of established authority. This is because they have little respect for laws or the authority figures that make them. As a result, people who habitually use antisocial behaviors tend to be loners operating outside the mainstream of society or in isolated subcultures.

Many people live lives of apparent social respectability while habitually using antisocial behaviors. There are apparently successful business people, for example, who consistently commit crimes and use their business as a front. These underground antisocials live a lifestyle of apparent respectability while privately and irresponsibly violating the law and skillfully manipulating and victimizing others for personal gain. They often have positions of power and try to use their influence to manipulate the laws and avoid capture or punishment.

39

*Antisocial behaviors are any actions that irresponsibly defy established laws, morality, or a sense of justice and fair play.*

Antisocial behaviors are not to be confused with responsible acts of protest against unjust laws or tyrannical authority figures. Many people protest against and, at times, defy laws on moral, religious, or political grounds. Their motives and styles of defiance are very different from those of people who commit antisocial acts. They typically protest openly, have a valid moral or ethical position behind their stance, and use the legally sanctioned mechanisms of protest to lever the change. If they feel morally compelled to violate what they perceive as immoral or unjust laws, they do so in a way that does not victimize others and accept responsibility for the consequences of their defiance of law and leadership. Many leaders such as Gandhi and Martin Luther King, Jr., defied many unjust laws but would not be described as antisocial.

People using antisocial behavior, in contrast, are generally self-serving, victimize others, defy authority without a firm basis in ethical or moral values, and expect to get away with it or to be held harmless from any adverse consequences. They rarely use socially acceptable routes of protest. They are interested in self-gain, not in making a positive contribution to society. Most people who habitually use antisocial behaviors posture themselves as good people who are being victimized by an unjust society. Upon clear examination, however, it is discovered that they are victimizers who are routinely violating the rights of others for personal gain and expect to get away with it. They tend to view anyone who attempts to interfere with their victimization of others as wrong or unjust. They feel entitled to do what they want, when they want, without being held accountable for the consequences of their behavior.

By this definition nearly 100 percent of all criminal offenders commit antisocial acts. Nearly 75 percent would be defined as habitual criminals who repeatedly engage in antisocial behavior despite adverse consequences. Most of these habitual criminals have a personality style we will call criminal.

## Defining the Terms

To understand the concept of antisocial behavior and expand that into a concept of a criminal personality style, we have to define the terms personality, personality trait, personality style, self-defeating personality style, and personality disorder.

**Personality** is a set of enduring and deeply entrenched habits of perceiving, thinking, feeling, acting, and relating to self, others, and the world. A habit is something that we do automatically and without thinking. Each personality style has distinctive differences in each of these five habits and, as a result of these differences in habitual response, each style functions differently when interacting with the world. Because personality consists of five distinctive habits, any effective approach to personality change must address all five habits of personality.

Personality is developed in childhood and is often unconsciously repeated in adulthood. Personality results from a complex interaction between genetically inherited temperaments and early childhood experiences. Most psychologists agree that personality is firmly formed by the time a child reaches age ten. Others argue that the major determinants of personality are firmly entrenched by age five.

Personality is also affected by *transformational adult experiences*. Some of these transformational experiences can

41

produce positive personality change. Others can produce negative or debilitating personality change. It is important to explore a person's life history to identify the key events that have influenced the personality either in a positive or negative way.

A **personality trait** is a single aspect or characteristic of the personality. The tendency to be hard working and compulsive, for example, would be a personality trait. Other personality traits could include the tendency to be active, passive, independent, dependent, or ambivalent. To be called a personality trait, a characteristic must appear in many different areas of a person's life and be characteristic or descriptive of the person's general way of being or operating in the world. These traits become the building blocks or individual components of a person's overall personality style.

Isolated behaviors not part of a characteristic pattern should not be confused with personality traits. Some people, for example, may exhibit anger whenever dealing with a specific person but are not angry people in general. Others may become submissive or docile whenever dealing with their mothers but would not be generally described as docile or submissive people. These isolated behaviors are not part of the general personality style.

A **personality style** is a pattern of personality traits. The person tends to exhibit a cluster of similar and related responses in many different situations and areas of his or her life. The situation does not dictate or govern the response. The response is determined by deeply entrenched habits of thinking, feeling, acting, and relating to others that are used across many different life areas. For example, someone with a passive personality style would tend to act in a reserved or withheld manner when dealing with most people. In contrast, someone with an oppositional personality style would tend to resist or fight against almost everyone he or she comes in contact with.

Personality styles can be healthy, self-defeating, or disordered. People with *healthy personality styles* tend to feel good and function well in the world. They are able to live effectively and successfully get their needs met. Healthy personality traits are flexible, adaptive, and functional. People with *flexible personality traits* are able to change and adapt to new experiences and situations. They can learn from the past, apply the new knowledge to the current situation, and respond in new, more effective ways. People with *adaptive personalities* are capable of adjusting to meet current needs. They are not locked into certain repetitive patterns. They can change as required by the situation. People with *functional personality styles* are able to use their personalities to produce desired outcomes. Functional people get things done in a way that does not create unnecessary problems for themselves or others.

---

### Personality Styles

**Functional**
- *Feel good, function well*

**Self-defeating**
- *Feel bad, function adequately*

**Disordered**
- *Feel bad, function poorly*

---

People with **self-defeating personality styles** tend to feel bad but function adequately. Their personality creates constant problems and, although they are able to meet their basic survival needs, they usually fail to get what they want out of life. As a result, they are usually unhappy and live in a state of chronic, low-grade emergency. A self-defeating personality style, therefore, is a specific set of personality traits that doesn't allow the people who have them to get what they want out of life. In other words, they have habitual ways of thinking, managing their feelings, behaving, and relating to others that sets them up to fail.

43

Self-defeating personalities are inflexible, maladaptive, and dysfunctional. They are inflexible because they are rigid and unchangeable. The person cannot adjust or adapt to new circumstances and has difficulty learning from the past and putting that new knowledge into practice in the current situation. They are *maladaptive* because they cannot adjust or respond to meet the new needs or demands of their environment. They are *dysfunctional* because they do not produce the desired outcomes and create unnecessary problems.

People with **personality disorders** tend to feel bad and function poorly. They repeatedly use irrational thinking and self-defeating behaviors that result in the development of physical, psychological, and social problems. People with a personality disorder will defend and maintain the self-defeating style despite the serious problems and consequences. They perceive themselves as doing well and functioning normally. They usually have little insight into the self-defeating nature of their own behavior. They are usually not receptive to feedback and think that anyone who tells them that they have a problem is being overly critical and unfair. They often blame others for the problems that are created by their own personalities.

Personality disorders are extremely rigid, self-defeating personality styles that consistently produce *subjective distress* ("I feel bad on the inside"), *social impairment* ("I can't function on the outside"), and *occupational impairment* ("I can't function on the job"). People with personality disorders cannot live normally, maintain employment or productive work relationships, or make intimate or family relationships work. They have trouble getting along with people and often come into conflict with the society. In the terms of DSM-IIIR, they experience "social and occupation impairments" as a consequence of their personality styles.

Many people with personality disorders end up in serious

44

conflict with society—in jail or accessing social welfare programs. Often, despite honest offers of help from society, they are unwilling or unable to change their behavior and learn the skills necessary to function effectively in society. *When you have a personality disorder, your own personality is your biggest enemy.*

*Criminal personality disorders* are extremely self-defeating personality styles that result in compulsive and chronic rule breaking, defiance of authority, extreme egotistical and self-centered behavior, disruptive attention seeking, and chaotic and volatile acting-out behavior.

The standard manual for classifying personality disorders is the *Diagnostic and Statistical Manual IIIR* (DSM-IIIR) of the American Psychiatric Association (1987). This manual describes three separate categories or clusters of personality disorders. Cluster A personality disorders describe people who appear odd or eccentric and have difficulty fitting into the established social structure. Cluster B personality disorders describe people who appear dramatic, emotional, and erratic and who tend to be overtly manipulative, controlling, and disruptive. Cluster C personality disorders describe people who appear anxious and fearful and tend to be passive, quietly controlling, and victimized by others.

## DSM-IIIR Personality Disorders

| Cluster A | Cluster B | Cluster C |
|---|---|---|
| *Appear odd or eccentric* | *Appear dramatic, emotional, or erratic* | *Appear anxious and fearful* |
| 1. Paranoid | 1 Antisocial | 1. Avoidant |
| 2. Schizoid | 2. Narcissistic | 2. Dependent |
| 3. Schizotypal | 3. Histrionic | 3. Obsessive/Compulsive |
| | 4. Borderline | 4. Passive/Aggressive |

Chronic and habitual criminals tend to have Cluster B personality disorders or tend to be Cluster C personality disorders who align themselves as passive victims of a person with a Cluster B criminal personality disorder and then repeatedly commit crimes under the instruction of the person with the criminal personality. In this book, the term criminal personality will be used to describe people with Cluster B personality traits or disorders. The term *criminally codependent* will be used to describe people with Cluster C personality traits or disorders who are in a dependent relationship with a person with a criminal personality and is manipulated to commit crimes.

| Criminal Personality | Criminally Codependent Personality |
|---|---|
| 1. Cluster B personality traits | 1. Cluster C personality traits |
| 2. Actively involved in criminal or antisocial behavior | 2. Antisocially curious |
| 3. Uses other people as an extension of criminal behavior | 3. In manipulative relationship with partner with ASPD |

Although both men and women can have either a criminal personality or a criminally codependent personality, criminal personality disorders are most common among male offenders and criminally codependent personality disorders are most common among women offenders.

Our primary focus will be on understanding criminal personality disorders, especially the antisocial personality disorder. This is because this set of criminal personality traits has been most extensively researched. The criminally codependent style will also be discussed for two reasons. First, it is commonly seen among women offenders. Second, most people with criminal personalities develop intimate relationships with people with criminally codependent personalities. Unless these significant others are treated, they will inadvertently contribute to the relapse of their partners.

People with personality disorders have a mental illness. They need treatment in the form of psychotherapy that will help them to break their denial and recognize the self-defeating set of behaviors that are preventing them from getting what they want out of life.

Unfortunately, one of the common symptoms of personality disorders is denial. People with personality disorders often perceive themselves as normal and put the blame for their problems on someone else. They believe, "I'm fine and everyone else has problems!" This denial prevents them from seeking treatment until they are forced to do so. When they enter treatment they often have high levels of resistance.

## The Continuum of Personality Problems

As can be seen, there is a continuum of personality problems ranging from mild to severe. Even people with basically *healthy personalities* will experience mild problems from time to time. People who are habitually experiencing minor and irritating problems because of their personality have *self-defeating personality traits*. Those who have such severe problems that they can't function normally are said to have *personality disorders*. It is important to keep this continuum in mind to properly assess how severe your client's personality problems are.

## Treating Personality Problems

**Psychotherapy** is a specific treatment designed to change personality. Most forms of psychotherapy consist of teaching people how to identify and change their rigid patterns of self-defeating thinking, feeling management, and behaviors. This is done by teaching clients about the personality style

47

they have, showing them why their personality is not working for them, and teaching them about healthy personality traits that they can develop to correct the problems. The client is then guided in a self-evaluation of his or her own personality style and asked to decide if it is healthy or self-defeating. The client is asked to make a commitment to change by identifying and modifying the specific self-defeating patterns of perceiving, thinking, feeling, acting, and relating that are causing problems. Strategies for changing these habitual ways of being need to be developed, and long-term support and reinforcement for new and more effective ways of being must be provided.

## The Criminal Personality Styles

DSM-IIIR identifies four Cluster B personality styles that are often seen in criminal offenders. These are: (1) antisocial, (2) narcissistic, (3) histrionic, and (4) borderline. The antisocial style is marked by compulsive rule breaking. The narcissistic style is marked by egotistical and self-centered behavior. The histrionic style is marked by disruptive and self-defeating attention seeking. The borderline style is marked by chaotic, volatile behavior and extreme unpredictable mood swings. In other works, I have used the term **counterdependent personality** to describe people with Cluster B personality styles and disorders (Gorski, 1993).

It is important to remember that people may have individual criminal personality traits without having full-blown personality disorders. Some people, for example, may defy authority in a narrow area of their lives but be socially conforming in *ex:* other areas. Others will routinely and without conscience break intimate commitments to lovers and spouses but would never consider stealing or being dishonest in a business transaction. Still others cheat on their income tax and commit "white collar crimes" but would never consciously break a traffic law.

Other people have self-defeating criminal personality traits that are noticeable but are not rigid or severe enough to get them into serious trouble. Still others have severe and rigid criminal personalities that constantly compel them to violate the rights of others, break the law, and be apprehended and prosecuted within the criminal justice system. These people frequently get into trouble with the law and make up the mainstream of the criminal justice system. This book focuses on people who abuse alcohol and drugs and also have serious criminal personality traits that motivate repeated criminal behavior.

## Personality Disorders as a Biopsychosocial Disease

This question naturally arises: Why do people keep doing all of these self-defeating things when they keep getting in trouble as a result? To answer that question we need to examine criminal personality as a biopsychosocial disorder. "Bio" refers to the biological or physical components of criminal personality. There appears to be a number of genetically inherited traits that influence brain function strongly associated with antisocial or criminal behavior. "Psycho" refers to the psychological components or the learned habits of thinking, managing feelings, and behaving that lock people into repetitive criminal patterns. "Social" refers to the established relationships at home and with friends, family, and lovers that reinforce antisocial behavior. All three levels of symptoms interact to lock many criminal offenders into repetitively and self-destructive patterns of crime that destroy their lives and damage society.

==

## Personality Is Biopsychosocial

**Bio = Biological (of the body)**
- Genetically influenced preferences

**Psycho = Psychological (of the mind)**
- Habits of thinking, managing feelings, and acting

**Social = Relationships (of society)**
- Work, social, and intimate networks that support the personality

========================================

## Biological Aspects of Criminal Personality

Many people with criminal personality traits have geneti-cally influenced brain dysfunction that predisposes them to self-centered and antisocial behavior. To understand this notion we must first recognize that all personality traits are influenced by genetics. We are all born with genetically influenced traits. There are four major traits that are influential in determining the direction of personality: active vs. passive; independent vs. dependent; inner directed vs. outer directed; and thinking oriented vs. feeling oriented. Let's look at each of these preferences in more detail.

**Active and Passive Traits:** People who are active tend to have a high energy level. They are energy generators who transmit energy from themselves to the things and people around them. People who are passive tend to be energy absorbers. They draw energy from the people around them into themselves. They tend to feel low energy and need to be stimulated by the people and things around them. *People with criminal personalities and criminally codependent personalities tend to be active and high energy.*

**Independent and Dependent Traits:** People who are independent tend to rely on themselves and have difficulty relying on or trusting others. They want to stand on their own two feet without depending on anyone else. People who are

50

dependent prefer to rely on other people. They like reassurance and prefer that someone else tell them what to do and take responsibility if something goes wrong. *People with criminal personalities tend to be fiercely independent. People with criminally codependent personalities tend to be very dependent.*

---

### Criminal Personality Is Biopsychosocial
**Bio = Biological (of the body)**
- Brain functioning that predisposes to self-centered and antisocial behavior

**Psycho = Psychological (of the mind)**
- Personality constructed around antisocial thrill seeking and pathological independence

**Social = Relationships (of society)**
- Lifestyle preferences that support antisocial behavior

---

**Outer-directed and Inner-directed Traits:** People who are outer directed feel most comfortable in the external world. They are often described as extroverts and tend to focus outside of themselves on people and things. They have a difficult time getting centered inside their own skin and find it difficult to recognize and manage their inner experiences. They don't like to introspect and, when under pressure, tend to run away from the inner experiences by getting overly involved with people and things in their outer world. People who are inner directed are called introverts and feel the most comfortable with their inner experiences. They enjoy attending to their inner thoughts, fantasies, and feelings. They are not very comfortable in the external world and, when under pressure, retreat to their private inner world. *People with criminal personalities tend to be extroverted and enjoy controlling external people and events. People with criminally* *codependent personalities tend to be introverted and want to be left alone to enjoy their private inner experiences.*

**Thinking and Feeling Traits:** Thinkers feel at home in a world of ideas and concepts. They are good at figuring things out, identifying patterns, and seeing the underlying principles that make things happen. Thinkers like to know what makes things happen and what the meaning is behind what happens. Feelers, on the other hand, are more comfortable having experiences, and they tend to avoid trying to figure out what experiences mean. They enjoy intensity for its own sake and don't spend a lot time figuring out what the experiences mean. Thinkers enjoy figuring things out and tend to dislike intense experiences that interfere with clear thought. Feelers enjoy intense experiences and tend to dislike trying to explain and figure out what the experiences mean. *People with both criminal personalities and criminally codependent personalities tend to be feelers who want intense experiences in the moment without having to think things through or figure out why they are doing things and what the consequences will be.*

People with criminal personalities tend to surround themselves with people who have criminally codependent personalities. Those with a criminally codependent personality have a high level of antisocial curiosity but are very dependent and lack the capacity to act out this curiosity without strong encouragement and support. They are attracted to antisocials and are fascinated by crime and criminal behaviors. Their high levels of energy and high activity levels make them perfect accomplices to crime. Their dependency makes them vulnerable to being manipulated by people with criminal personalities. Their feeling orientation and general difficulty with thinking things through cause them to get caught up in the excitement of the moment and make it difficult for them to

52

project the logical consequences of what they are doing or to learn from past experiences.

A large percentage of male offenders will have criminal personality styles and be in relationships with people with criminally codependent personality styles. A large percentage of women offenders will have criminally codependent personality styles and be in a relationship with people with criminal personalities who are exploiting them.

## The Genetic Underpinnings of Antisocial Personality

There are five genetic predispositions that may be associated with antisocial personality disorder. These are: high sensation seeking, poor impulse control, preference for concrete thinking, difficulty with abstract and symbolic learning, and insensitivity to others due to self-absorption.

---

### Genetic Predisposition for Criminal Personality Disorder

- High sensation seeking
- Poor impulse control
- Preference for concrete thinking
- Difficulty with abstract and symbolic reasoning
- Insensitivity to others due to self-absorption

---

People with **high sensation-seeking tendencies** have a preference for exciting activities that produce an adrenaline rush. They are easily bored and crave a variety of intensely stimulating activities. People with **poor impulse control** overreact to external stimulation and have difficulty resisting self-defeating impulses.

People who have a **preference for concrete thinking** and have **difficulty with abstract and symbolic reasoning** tend to deal with the immediate concrete realities. If they can't touch it, take a picture of it, or put it in a box, they have difficulty understanding and dealing with it.

People who are **insensitive to others** tend to be self-absorbed, perceive people as objects, and feel justified in using people in an impersonal way to get what they want.

Look at the deadly relationship between these preferences. I am a high-sensation seeker who craves excitement but, when I get into intense situations, I lose control of myself and end up doing things that get me into trouble as a result of my poor impulse control. I sense that something is wrong, but I have difficulty figuring it out because I prefer thinking in concrete terms and have trouble with abstract thinking processes that would help me see the pattern of what is going on. Because I tend to be insensitive to others and self-absorbed, I either don't notice or don't care about how people respond or react to me. As a result, it is easy for me to hurt people and not even notice or care about it. Here in a nutshell is a description of a person with antisocial tendencies.

Many people get concerned because I describe these traits as biological preference. They tend to assume that because a certain mode of behavior is biologically more comfortable that people "have to" act it out. This is not true. People can learn to overcome or modify biologically preferred behaviors. It is difficult to do so, but it is possible. Many people with these traits never commit a crime or an antisocial act because starting as little children their parents helped them to learn how to redirect and compensate for these tendencies in the personality. Unfortunately, many others were raised in childhood environments that reinforced these dynamics. These people often develop deeply entrenched criminal personality traits.

## The Biological Dynamics of Criminal Personality Disorder

Let's look at how these biologically influenced traits can dynamically interact with each other to lock a person into a cycle of acting out behavior. The following diagram shows the biological dynamics that may underlie criminal personality patterns.

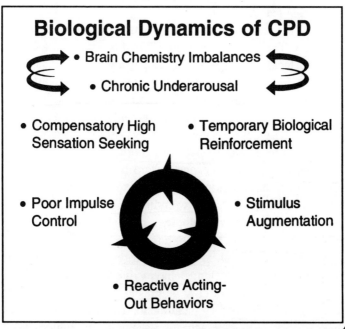

**Biological Dynamics of CPD**

- Brain Chemistry Imbalances
- Chronic Underarousal
- Compensatory High Sensation Seeking
- Temporary Biological Reinforcement
- Poor Impulse Control
- Stimulus Augmentation
- Reactive Acting-Out Behaviors

The person who is genetically predisposed to criminal personality may be born with a brain chemistry imbalance. The theory is that such individuals have deficiencies in brain chemicals necessary to maintain normal states of energy and attention. This biological condition results in a state of constant or chronic underarousal. These persons feel low energy and lethargic, and they have difficulty concentrating and focusing their energy.

*[handwritten margin notes: How does diet — i.o. sugar — destiny to balance predispose persons to chemical addiction? Other]*

To overcome this state of underarousal or low energy, the person engages in **compensatory sensation seeking**. He or she is drawn toward activities that are highly stimulating and that create a rush of adrenaline. These activities temporarily stabilize the brain chemistry, and the feeling of underarousal or low energy is temporarily relieved. This behavior is said to be **biologically reinforcing** because it produces a pleasant or enjoyable reaction in the body.

Now the tendency toward **poor impulse control** comes into play. The person is engaging in highly stimulating behavior and lacks the capacity or skill to moderate or stop the activity. In other words they can't control their impulses to act out. This leads to **reactive acting-out behavior**. The person gets caught up in the excitement of the moment and keeps doing what feels good regardless of the consequences. This leads to a state of overexcitability known as **stimulus augmentation**. The nervous system begins overreacting to the stress of the situation, creating an excess of adrenaline and other stress chemicals. This produces a surge of energy that provides **temporary biological reinforcement**. In other words, it feels really good for a few minutes.

Unfortunately, nothing good lasts forever. When the person stops the sensation-seeking behavior, the brain rapidly returns to its previous state of chronic underarousal and the person becomes restless and agitated again. This motivates him or her to seek out other sensation-seeking experiences once again to gain relief, and the cycle starts all over again. The end result is an escalating pattern of excitement-seeking behavior that eventually gets out of control. This can lead to criminal behavior, especially when the excitement-seeking behavior is enhanced with the use of alcohol or other drugs, which further lowers impulse control and distorts judgment.

People with criminal personalities have difficulty recognizing and changing this pattern for a number of reasons. First, they have a preference for concrete "here and now" thinking that keeps their attention focused on the immediate situation only. As a result they don't step back and look at the big picture. They just keep doing what feels good at that moment. Second, they have difficulty with abstract and symbolic learning, which prevents them from detecting the core issues and repetitive patterns they are locked into. Finally, they are insensitive to others and as a result tend to block out or disregard feedback from others.

This cycle creates biological reinforcement as a result of the intense euphoria and mood alteration from criminal thinking and sexual thrill seeking. It also causes high stress tolerance, and the person gets used to these intense experiences and learns how to enjoy and thrive on them. These people also have hangover resistance. They are able to rapidly recover or spring back from the aftermath of episodes that produce excessive stress.

If this model is correct, antisocial behavior in a genetically predisposed person can be seen as a trigger that activates positive mood changes, dependence and loss of control, and progressive social and occupational problems.

An important part of treating people with criminal personality traits is to explain this pattern to them so they can identify the repetitive self-defeating pattern they are locked into. They can then see the need for a holistic health program that includes proper diet, aerobic exercise, and stress management to help stabilize the brain and keep them out of the state of chronic underarousal that initiates the cycle. They also need to learn how to break out of this cycle when it gets started.

## The Psychological Aspects of Criminal Personality

As a biopsychosocial disorder, criminal personality also has a number of psychological traits associated with it. People who are predisposed to develop a criminal personality tend to center their mental and emotional life around antisocial thrill seeking and pathological independence. Antisocial thrill seeking involves the excitement produced by acting out criminally and sexually. Pathological independence involves the belief that "I can stand on my own and do what I want without regarding or needing anyone else." There are basically six psychological traits associated with criminal personality.

---

### Addictive Personality Characteristics

**1. Obsession**
- Out-of-control thinking about antisocial thrill seeking

**2. Compulsion**
- Irrational urge to engage in antisocial thrill seeking despite adverse consequences

**3. Loss of Behavioral Control**
- Inability to resist urges to use antisocial behavior

**4. Personality Change**
- Altered values, attitudes, and beliefs as a result of living an antisocial lifestyle

**5. Secondary Life Problems**
- Lifestyle problems caused by use

**6. Denial of Addiction**
- View of self as an innocent victim of an unfair world

---

The first psychological trait is **obsession** or out-of-control thinking about antisocial thrill seeking. The person spends more and more time thinking about and fantasizing about antisocial and illegal acts.

The second trait is **compulsion** or the irrational urge to engage in antisocial thrill seeking despite adverse consequences. The person with a criminal personality feels an urge or a compulsion to act in antisocial ways. This compulsion is irrational and can at times be so strong that it is overpowering. The third trait is **loss of behavioral control** or the inability to resist urges to use antisocial behavior. These people begin using antisocial behaviors even though they know that they will get into trouble. In essence, they can't stop themselves.

The fourth trait is **personality change** or the change in values, attitudes, and beliefs that occurs as a result of constant obsession with antisocial behavior. These people are so pre-occupied with preparing for, committing, and avoiding capture for the antisocial acts they commit that other aspects of their personal development are ignored and neglected.

The fifth trait is **secondary life problems**, which include legal, social, and occupational problems caused by the criminal and antisocial behavior. People with criminal personalities are constantly experiencing problems of all kinds. Their antisocial behavior creates the problems, and then they use the problems as an excuse to commit more antisocial acts. It is not uncommon to hear a criminal offender say, "If it weren't for all these problems in my life, I would never have committed a crime!" They cannot see or admit that, if they hadn't committed hundreds of antisocial acts, they never would have developed the problems that they use as an excuse to commit new crimes.

The sixth trait is **denial of criminal personality**. People with criminal personality traits tend to view themselves as innocent victims of an unfair world. They feel that they have a right to do what they want, when they want, without regard to the rights or well-being of others. When the consequences of their behaviors cause problems, they accept little or no responsibility and tend to blame the victim or the enforcer. The typical rationale is, "If the victim hadn't screamed so loud, I wouldn't be here!" or, "If the cop hadn't arrested me [*or the judge hadn't sentenced me*], I wouldn't be here. I had nothing to do with it!"

You will notice that these traits are similar to those present in chemical dependency, but the focus is different. Chemically dependent people are obsessed and feel a compulsion to use alcohol and drugs. People with criminal personality are obsessed with a compulsion to use criminal and sexual thrill-seeking behaviors. People with both disorders are preoccupied with both sets of symptoms.

## The Social Aspects of Criminal Personality

Criminal personality has a number of social symptoms that support antisocial or criminal behavior. These social symptoms show up as a cluster of lifestyle preferences that reinforce the continued use of antisocial or criminal behaviors. There are four primary social symptoms.

The first social symptom is an **antisocial and isolated lifestyle**. People with criminal personality styles view themselves as loners and rugged individualists. The consequences of their antisocial behavior make it difficult for them to get along with other people. They rationalize this as "not liking others" or that "other people aren't healthy enough or strong enough to get along with someone like me!"

---

### Social Symptoms of Criminal Personality
1. Antisocial and Isolated Lifestyle
2. Unstable Work History
3. Intimate Relationship Problems
   - Sexual exploitation
   - No emotional bonding
4. Friendship Problems
   - Short term
   - Mutually exploitive

---

The second symptom is an **unstable work history**. People with severe criminal personality traits have difficulty keeping jobs or maintaining steady employment. They typically don't value work. They believe that working for a living is for chumps or losers. They pride themselves on believing that they can beat the system and get something for nothing. They also have difficulty following rules and deferring to authority figures. As a result they tend to move from job to job and have long periods of unemployment.

People with criminal personality styles also have **intimate relationship problems**. They tend to sexualize all intimacy and then turn people into sexual objects to exploit and abuse. They lack a willingness or capacity for emotional bonding and often want their sexual relationships to be impersonal and one way: "I want you to reinforce me sexually and meet my needs, but you have no right to expect the same from me!"

People with antisocial personalities also have **friendship problems**. They don't value friends. They believe that people are there to be used and manipulated. Most of their friendships are short term because they lack the willingness or capacity to negotiate and maintain relationships over a long period of time. Friendships that they do have are not friendships at all. They are distant acquaintances or periodic companionships typically centered around mutual exploitation or shared criminal or sexual thrill seeking.

## The Progression of Criminal Personality

Criminal personality tends to progress as the symptoms escalate and the person loses the ability to control or self-regulate the impulse to act out. This progression can be viewed as unfolding in four predictable stages: prodromal, early, middle, and chronic.

## The Progressive Stages
### of
### Criminal Personality Disorder

**Prodromal Stage:** Fascination and experimentation with antisocial criminal and sexual thrill seeking

**Early Stage:** Growing dependency on antisocial behavior for identity and mood regulation

**Middle Stage:** Progressive loss of control

**Chronic Stage:** Deterioration

During the **prodromal stage,** the person with a tendency toward criminal personality becomes fascinated with and begins to experiment with antisocial criminal and sexual thrill seeking. Here the environmental response is critical. If the person is in a subculture that reinforces this behavior, it rapidly progresses. If, on the other hand, the person is in a rigid environment that condemns any form of excitement seeking or alternative lifestyle patterns, he or she tends to go underground and escalate the acting out. If the behavior is recognized early and redirected into socially acceptable forms of thrill seeking and the person receives moral guidance and training in how to manage impulses, the progression can be stopped before it starts. Because these tendencies are normally present in childhood, the reactions of parents and teachers are critical at this stage. At each stage of recovery, the type and level of support for the immediate social environment is very important.

The **early stage** is marked by a growing dependency on antisocial behavior for identity and mood regulation. These people come to see themselves as rebels or criminals who have little regard for the law or the authorities who make laws. They take pride in seeing themselves as rugged individualists who are above the law and have a right to use and abuse others.

They have glorified role models of antisocial people and build their identity around these role models. They also get in the habit of using sexual and criminal thrill seeking to manage their moods. When they feel bad, they find that acting out can make them feel better. They use it frequently and fail to learn other ways of managing their feelings and inner experiences.

The **middle stage** is marked by a progressive loss of control over the ability to self-regulate criminal behaviors. During this stage offenders try to cut back on criminal behaviors. They begin getting into trouble and doing things they regret later. They go through periods of time when they swear off crime and antisocial behavior and may even go to the other extreme by becoming a "fundamentalist do-gooder." In the end, however, they return to antisocial behavior.

The **chronic stage** is marked physical, psychological, and social deterioration. The antisocial lifestyle begins to take its toll. Physical health suffers because of excessive stress, accidents, and injuries incurred while committing antisocial acts. Psychological health begins to suffer. The person fluctuates between criminal grandiosity ("I am lord in absolute control and I must always have my way!") to zero-state thinking ("I am nothing, I will always be nothing, and everyone knows it!"). In this state, the criminal often alternates between grandiosity and criminal acting out and severe depression and suicidal ideation. Socially the person has become alienated and isolated with little hope and few prospects.

It is important to point out that biologically predisposed people who use antisocial thinking and behavior in a socially reinforcing environment often develop progressive antisocial personality traits. Social and environmental factors can accelerate or retard this progression. In other words, if a person is in an environment that supports and reinforces antisocial behavior, the progression will occur more rapidly. If the person is in an environment that discourages antisocial behavior and offers other alternatives outlets for high sensation seeking tendencies, the progression can be slowed or reversed. As a result, environmental constraints are necessary for change.

---

**Criminal Personality**
**The Long-term Outcomes**

- Life-long incarceration
- Crippling injury or death during antisocial acting out
- Suicide
- Recovery

---

There are just a few possible long-term alternatives for people with criminal personality disorders: life-long incarceration, crippling injury, or death during antisocial acting out (or suicide). The only other alternative is to get treatment and make a commitment to recovery. Unfortunately, few people with criminal personality disorders will voluntary initiate treatment. Referrals must be mandated and enforced. The good news is that treatment alternatives for mandated offenders can be effective.

## DSM-IIIR Criteria for Antisocial Personality Disorder

For people to meet the criteria for the Antisocial Personality Disorder list in the DSM-IIIR, they must meet two general criteria: (1) they must have had a **conduct disorder** before age fifteen; and (2) they must have had a **pattern of antisocial behavior** since age fifteen.

To meet the criteria for having a conduct disorder before age fifteen, they must have three or more of the following twelve criteria:

- Frequent truancy
- Overnight runaway (twice or more)
- Initiated physical fights
- Use of weapon (more than once)
- Forced sexual activity
- Physical cruelty to animals
- Physical cruelty to people
- Vandalism and destruction of property
- Deliberate fire setting
- Frequent lying
- Theft without victim confrontation
- Theft with victim confrontation

To meet the criteria for having a pattern of antisocial behavior since the age of fifteen, the person must have four or more of the following:

1. Inconsistent pattern of work or academic behavior
   - Unemployment when able to work and work is available
   - Unexcused absences and tardiness
   - Irresponsible job abandonment
2. Law breaking and violations of social norms (whether arrested or not)
3. Irritable and aggressive
   - Physical fights and assaults
   - Child or spouse beating
4. Default on financial obligations
   - Failure to pay back debts
   - Failure to pay for support of dependents
5. Impulsive, fails to plan ahead
   - Prolonged aimless traveling
   - No fixed address for more than one month
6. Dishonest, no regard for the truth
   - Repeated lying
   - Use of aliases
   - Conning for profit or pleasure

7. Reckless behavior that endangers self or others
   - Driving while intoxicated
   - Speeding and reckless driving
8. Irresponsible parenting
   - Malnutrition of child
   - Child's illness resulting from lack of hygiene
   - Failure to provide medical care for seriously ill child
   - Failure to provide food or clothing
   - Failure to arrange child care
   - Repeated squandering of money required for household necessities
9. Never sustained monogamous relationship for more than a year
10. Lacks remorse
    - Feels justified in antisocial behaviors
    - Blames victims for offenses

## The Manipulative Personality— Functional Antisocials

The term *antisocial personality* is too limiting to describe all people who have similar personality traits. Many people are driven by the same biological, psychological, and social imperatives as antisocials but would never be labeled as such because they act out in manipulative and abusive yet socially conforming ways. Many business executives, for example, rise to power through a series of brutal and antisocial acts that don't technically break any laws. There are accounts of political leaders who have attempted to or actually changed laws to make their antisocial behavior acceptable.

Sometimes I think that a better name for antisocial personality would be the *manipulative personality* with two subtypes: social conforming and antisocial. The primary personality dynamics of both are based on a common foundation. Both are driven people who navigate a complex bio-

66

logical cycle that leads from boredom and understimulation to a craving for excitement, and then into an overreactive and hyperexcitable mode. This is followed by a crash, which motivates the cycle to begin all over again. Both also have a deep-seated disrespect for authority, power fantasies, and the need to be in absolute control. Both are capable of turning others into objects and then using them for personal pleasure or gain. Both tend to be loners who alienate others and end up isolated and alone.

The major difference is the way these tendencies are acted out and the arena in which they choose to act out these tendencies. The socially conforming manipulative personality will stay within the letter of the law while using and abusing others for personal gain. The antisocial manipulative personality will be fascinated with criminality and seek overtly illegal avenues to act out.

Sometimes the critical factor is access to opportunity. An antisocial personality at the Harvard Business School is far more likely to act out in socially conforming ways than a street kid in the ghetto whose only avenues of economic success are drug dealing and crime.

It is important to recognize that most people in prison are from minority groups and lower socioeconomic levels of society. This appears to occur for several reasons. First, poor families often cannot provide social and economic opportunities for their children that would allow them to redirect manipulative tendencies in a socially conforming way. Second, minorities and lower socioeconomic class people simply do not have ready access to upward mobility in society. Third, these people often suffer from discrimination and lack of legal options once arrested that would minimize their sentencing and keep them out of prison.

## Pseudo-antisocial Personality

Chemical dependency will often make people look antisocial when they really are not. Chemical dependency can also exaggerate antisocial traits and make people appear to be more criminal than they really are. When people are intoxicated their judgment and impulse control are severely impaired. As a result, they can engage in antisocial behaviors that are not typical of their normal personality when sober. Alcohol and drug withdrawal can have the same effect.

This is why it is important to get chemically dependent offenders thoroughly detoxified *before* making a definitive diagnosis. In a treatment program that I ran, we did personality tests on patients within the first several days of admission and again one month later. Nearly 80 percent of males and 40 percent of females showed serious antisocial personality traits on the first test. After thirty days of sobriety, the post-test showed that the majority had returned to more normal personality profiles.

The conclusion is that patients need to be thoroughly detoxified and stabilized before a definitive diagnosis of criminal personality disorder can be made.

## Criminal Personality Disorder—Basic Treatment Principles

Recovery from criminal personality disorder requires three things:

1. *Abstinence from antisocial behaviors and alcohol and drug use.* The most effective therapy for criminal personality traits focuses on modifying the criminal behavior itself. Therapies that fail to focus on the goal of abstinence from criminal behavior and deal exclusively with underlying psychological issues tend to fail in altering patterns of criminal behaviors. It is important to remember that chemical abuse and criminal personality are closely linked and any use of

68

alcohol and drugs, even in clients who are not chemically dependent, is strongly correlated with a relapse to antisocial and criminal behavior.

2. *Identifying and changing criminal thoughts, feelings, and lifestyle patterns*. Once a person is abstinent from the use of alcohol, drugs, and criminal behavior, the next step is to identify and change the patterns of criminal thinking, emotional management, and social functioning that drive the use of that behavior. The criminal behavior is the tip of the iceberg. The behavior is driven by deeply entrenched habits of thinking, feeling, and relating to others.

The specific thought that motivates criminal use must be identified, and the client must be taught to think in different ways. The emotional management style that requires criminal acting out needs to be identified and then new emotional coping strategies must be learned. Finally, the social network of friends, lovers, and companions which supports the lifestyle of crime must be changed. The person must learn to build a new social network that supports sobriety and responsibility.

3. *Deep personality and value change.* The primary goal of treatment is long-term change. For this to occur, people with criminal personality disorders must work on deep personality and value change. They must reorganize their basic view of themselves, other people, and the world. This will require long-term psychotherapy in a structured environment with continued accountability to assure that the offender does not drop out of treatment when the going gets rough.

## The Biopsychosocial Assessment Grid

To effectively treat chemically dependent criminal offenders, professionals must be able to quickly assess if the person has chemical dependency, criminal personality, or a combination of the two. The table on pages 70–71 summarizes the information that was presented in the first two chapters in a

| Biopsychosocial Assessment Grid (BAG) for Chemically Dependent Criminal Offenders | | |
| --- | --- | --- |
| Biopsychosocial Grid | Chemical Dependency (CD) | Criminal Personality Traits (CPT) |
| **1. Biological** | | |
| A. Genetic Predisposition | Metabolism of drug of choice makes it:<br>1. A powerful psychoactive medication<br>2. A cause of brain dysfunction | Brain chemistry imbalances cause:<br>High sensation seeking, poor impulse control, preference for concrete thinking, difficulty with abstract and symbolic learning, self-absorption and insensitivity |
| B. Biological Reinforcement | Use of the drug of choice produces:<br>1. Intense euphoria<br>2. Positive mood alteration | Criminal and sexual thrill seeking cause:<br>1. Intense euphoria<br>2. Mood alteration<br>3. Temporary personality change |
| C. High Tolerance | Heavy use of drug of choice without:<br>1. Intoxication<br>2. Dysfunctional | Long periods of intense excitement without:<br>1. Dysfunction during acute stress<br>2. Stress degeneration or burnout |
| D. Hangover Resistance | Rapid recovery from the adverse aftereffects using the drug of choice | Rapid recovery from the excessive stress of criminal thrill seeking |
| E. Brain Damage Sensitivity | Use of the drug of choice produces:<br>1. Increased immediate brain dysfunction<br>2. Prolonged recovery time<br>3. Progressive brain dysfunction | Not Applicable |
| **2. Psychological** | | |
| A. Higher Self | 1. Abstinent; critical and judgmental<br>2. Using: vivid and lucid | Disengages.<br>Lacks capacity for objective self-evaluation |
| B. Imaging | 1. Abstinent: repressed and inhibited<br>2. Using: vivid and lucid | Repressed and inhibited except when focused on criminal behavior |

| | |
|---|---|
| C. Perception | 1. Lock onto positive aspects of A/D use<br>2. Block out negative aspects of A/D use | 1. Lock onto positive aspects of criminality.<br>2. Block out negative aspects of criminality |
| D. Thinking | Addictive thinking patterns that protect<br>1. The right to use alcohol and drugs<br>2. Image of self as social drinker or recreational drug user despite evidence that A/D use is unsafe | Criminal thinking patterns that protect the right to act out in antisocial ways and the self-image of being a good person who is victimized by others despite evidence of victimizing others and destroying own life. |
| E. Feeling | Pattern of repression, overreaction, and remorse | Pattern of exaggeration, conversion to anger, acting out, and blaming others |
| F. Acting | Alcohol and drug-seeking behaviors involved in preparation for A/D use, use and recovery from the aftereffects of use | Criminal behaviors: Preparation, overcoming deterrents, acting out, and coping with the aftermath |
| 3. Social | | |
| A. Work | Occupational problems from loss of control over A/D use | Occupational problems from devaluation of work and conscious irresponsibility |
| B. Friendship | Friendship problems caused by A/D centered living and addictive isolation | Friendship problems caused by devaluation and manipulation, intrusive one-sided intimacy, and criminal isolation |
| C. Intimate/Sexual | A/D use interferes with the maintenance of intimate relationships | Intimacy problems caused by sexualizing all relationships and dominating, manipulating, and controlling all sexual partners |
| D. Family | A/D use that interferes with effectively meeting family responsibilities and roles | Voluntary withdrawal from and manipulation or abuse of family |
| E. Legal | Legal problems from intoxication and withdrawal that result in poor judgment, out-of-control behavior, and irresponsible behavior | Legal problems result from voluntary use of anti-social behaviors |

Developed by Terence T. Gorski (Copyright, T. Gorski, 1993)
The CENAPS Corporation, 18650 Dixie Highway, Homewood, IL 60430, 708-799-5000

way that allows quick and easy comparisons between the two disorders. This chart is called the Biopsychosocial Assessment Grid because it reviews the physical, psychological, and social symptoms of both chemical dependency and criminal personality in a simple and concise grid.

This grid can be used as an assessment or interview tool when dealing with clients. It can also be used as a handout and given to clients to reinforce material covered in individual, group, or educational sessions.

# Recovery fi
# Depend
# Criminal Personality
## A Developmental Model

Recovery from chemical dependency and criminal personality traits is a developmental process. The term "developmental" means to grow in steps or stages. Just as children have to learn how to crawl before they walk and how to walk before they run, chemically dependent criminal offenders have to learn a foundation of basic recovery skills before they are ready to move on to more advanced recovery skills.

Two **Developmental Models of Recovery** have been developed to describe the recovery process from chemical dependence. One model has been developed by Stephanie Brown (Brown, 1985) and the other model, The CENAPS Model, developed by Terence T. Gorski (Gorski, 1989). The CENAPS Model has been expanded and adapted to include the recovery process from criminal personality disorders (Mental Health in Corrections, 1993).

*Developmental* means to grow in steps or stages. A *model* is a way of thinking about and describing reality. *Recovery* means to get better. So a developmental model of recovery is a way of thinking about and describing recovery from chemical dependence and criminal personality traits as a series of steps or stages that a client goes through to get better.

There are six stages in the CENAPS Developmental Model of Recovery: Transition, Stabilization, Early Recovery, Middle Recovery, Late Recovery, and Maintenance. Each stage has a primary focus or recovery goal. Each stage also has a series of tasks that need to be completed.

The primary goal of **transition** is to recognize chemical dependency and criminal personality traits that are destroying their lives and to become willing to accept treatment.

The primary goal of stabilization is to stop using alcohol, drugs, and criminal behaviors and to recover from withdrawal and life crisis.

The primary goal of **early recovery** is to learn how to change patterns of addictive and criminal thinking, feeling, and behavior.

The primary goal of **middle recovery** is to repair past damage to the lifestyle caused by the use of alcohol, drugs, and criminal behavior.

The primary goal of **late recovery** is to change personality and values developed in childhood.

The primary goal of **maintenance** is to sustain an ongoing program of personal growth and development, guard against relapse, and responsibly deal with problems as they arise.

Let's look at each of these stages of recovery in more detail.

## Stage 1: Transition

During transition offenders recognize that they have serious problems resulting from the use of alcohol, drugs, and criminal behaviors. They make a decision to stop drinking, drugging, and committing crimes, and they become willing to seek help.

Transition consists of five basic tasks: (1) developing motivating problems; (2) attempting normal problem solving; (3) attempting to cut back or control; (4) attempting to stop without help; and (5) accepting help. Let's look at these in more detail.

---

Recovery Tasks of Transition
- Developing motivating problems
- Attempting normal problem solving
- Attempting to cut back or control
- Attempting to stop without help
- Accepting help

---

**Developing motivating problems:** People experience motivating problems when things begin to happen that prevent them from living their preferred lifestyle. Most chemically dependent criminal offenders have built their preferred lifestyle around drinking, drugging, and criminal thrill seeking. They would prefer to keep doing these things.

The trouble is that they begin having problems that interfere with this preferred lifestyle. They get arrested, get caught driving under the influence, overdose, or develop alcohol and drug-related problems. They may get hurt while committing a crime or have a close call with going to jail. Whatever the problem is, it convinces them that they need to do something different.

**Attempting normal problem solving:** Most offenders don't believe the problems they are exercising are related to their use of alcohol, drugs, and criminal behaviors. They have difficulty with abstract thinking and conceptualization so they view each motivating problem as something that is separate from and unrelated to their use of alcohol, drugs, and criminal behavior. As a result they typically attempt to solve the problems using their normal problem-solving processes.

How do alcoholics and drug addicts normally solve problems? They use alcohol and drugs to block them out or make them go away. How do criminals normally attempt to solve problems? They try to con, hustle, cheat, and lie their way out of them. As a result the problems usually get worse until the consequences become so severe that they see very clearly that they have to do something different.

**Attempt to cut back or control:** The first thing they try to do differently is to cut back or control their drinking, drugging, and criminal behavior. They know they have problems because they use too much of the wrong kind, too often. The solution is simple. Use less, of a different kind, less often. Still others work at controlling it. They switch from cocaine to marijuana, from bourbon to beer. They stop committing high-risk felonies and try to stick only to low-risk petty crimes. As one offender told me, "During this period I tried to lie only about the little things that didn't matter anyway."

They try to control their chemical use and criminal behaviors because they still believe they are social drinkers and recreational drug users who are basically good and responsible people who are being treated unfairly by their victims and the people appointed to enforce the laws.

These attempts to cut back or control normally fail, which forces their back against the wall. They are being confronted with undeniable evidence they are not social and recreational drinkers and drug users but out-of-control addicts. They are also forced to confront the fact they are not responsible people being victimized by others. They must realize that they are criminals who victimize others and have lost control of their criminal behaviors.

At this point offenders can see the handwriting on the wall. If they don't stop drinking, drugging, and committing crimes, their options are limited. They will either be incarcerated for life, die of alcohol and drug-related complications or accidents, get killed or crippled while committing crimes, or commit suicide.

**Attempt to stop without help:** Now the offenders are ready to stop using alcohol, drugs, and criminal behavior—at least for a little while. The problem is that they believe they can do it by themselves. They attempt to stop by just swearing off and telling themselves they will never use alcohol, drugs, or criminal behaviors again. The problem is that they can't keep that commitment. They inevitably end up returning to their old ways of dealing with life.

**Accepting help:** Now the offender has hit bottom and develops a desire to stop using alcohol, drugs, and criminal behaviors. They also develop a willingness to accept help, realizing they can't do it alone—but they are only temporarily willing to learn and follow directions. They feel desperate and are willing to go to any lengths to deal with the serious problems facing them.

**The relapse process during transition:** During the transition stage, chemically dependent criminal offenders tend to experience a classic pattern of relapse warning signs. First they develop *doubts about being addicted and having a criminal personality. They see that things are getting better and say to themselves, "Maybe it wasn't as bad as I thought. I think I overreacted. My problems weren't as bad as I thought they were. Look how good things are going now."*

Then they start using *euphoric recall*: euphoric means to feel good, and recall means to remember things. So euphoric recall is the process of remembering past experiences with alcohol, drugs, and criminal behaviors in a way that makes them feel good. They do this by remembering all of the good times and blocking out, minimizing, or romanticizing all of the pain and problems.

This is followed by *awfulizing sobriety and responsibility*. Sobriety is the process of living a meaningful, comfortable life without using alcohol and drugs. Responsibility is the process of living life without resorting to criminal behaviors to get what you want or need. When people awfulize recovery they begin to notice and exaggerate all the bad things that go along with being sober and responsible while blocking out any of the good things or benefits.

Then they begin to have *magical thinking about the use of alcohol, drugs, and criminal behaviors*. They start believing the only way to cope with life and solve problems is to drink, drug, and commit crimes. They believe that if only they could once again become a social drinker, recreational drug user, and successful criminal, their life would be wonderful.

This leads them into *obsession, compulsion, and craving*. Obsession is out-of-control thinking about the use of alcohol, drugs, and criminal behaviors. They spend more and more time thinking about the "good old days": how good it used to be, how awful it is that they can't use anymore, and how everything would be wonderful if only they could use again. They keep recycling these thoughts until they develop a powerful compulsion.

A compulsion is an irrational emotional urge to use alcohol, drugs, and criminal behavior even though they know that it is dangerous and not good for them to do it. This urge continues to grow until it becomes a full-blown craving. Many addicted criminals report that their whole body hurts for alcohol and drugs. They want it so bad they can taste it. They crave criminal thrill seeking and start to believe that nothing else can relieve the pain they are experiencing.

If the person can overcome these warning signs and complete the tasks of transition, he or she moves into early recovery.

## Stage 2: Stabilization

During stabilization, chemically dependent offenders stop using alcohol, drugs, and criminal behaviors and recover from withdrawal and life crisis.

Stabilization consists of five basic tasks: (1) using a structured recovery program; (2) stabilizing crisis; (3) breaking addictive and criminal preoccupation; (4) managing stress; and (5) developing hope and motivation. Let's look at these in more detail.

---

### Recovery Tasks of Stabilization
1. Using a structured recovery program
2. Stabilizing crisis
3. Breaking addictive and criminal preoccupation
4. Managing stress
5. Developing hope and motivation

---

**Using a structured recovery program:** It is important to remember that this willingness to accept help is usually linked to the problems they are experiencing. When life has you by the short hairs, your mind and heart will follow. But when the pressure is off and life returns to normal, the motivation to change and the willingness to accept help and follow directions often disappears.

This is why it is important to get a commitment to a long-term, structured recovery program. Chemically dependent offenders must be put in a situation where they can be held accountable for participating in a recovery program. Any time chemically dependent offenders start to feel better, their motivation tends to disappear and they feel an urge to drop out

79

of treatment. If this happens, there must be a way to create a new motivational crisis before a full-blown relapse occurs. The best way to do this is to make long-term treatment a condition of probation and parole and have definite legal consequences imposed any time the offenders break with their treatment program.

**Stabilizing crisis:** When chemically dependent people stop using alcohol, drugs, and criminal behaviors, things don't instantly get better. In fact, things often get worse before they start to get better. This is why many chemically dependent offenders have three types of presenting crises: withdrawal, the post-crime crash, and life crisis.

Alcohol and drug *withdrawal* plague chemically dependent offenders. When people become addicted, the body gets used to having high levels of alcohol and other drugs in the blood stream. The brain and body adapt to the presence of the drugs, and they learn how to function normally with the drugs in their system. Without the right amount in the blood stream, addicts get sick. This sickness is called *acute withdrawal.*

There is a longer-term withdrawal called *post acute withdrawal.* The word "post" means after. Post acute withdrawal refers to the withdrawal symptoms that appear after acute withdrawal has subsided. It is important to remember that alcohol and drugs damage the brain and that the brain takes a long time to heal. During the post acute withdrawal period, people have difficulty thinking clearly, managing their feelings and emotions, and remembering things. Under high stress they lose the ability to sleep restfully and may become accident prone. As they recover and stabilize, these symptoms get less and less severe until they often go away completely. To make the withdrawal symptoms go away, most chemically dependent people need medical help with withdrawal.

There is also a *post-crime crash.* When the criminal thrill-seeking behaviors are suddenly stopped, offenders feel anxious, irritable, and depressed. They are jittery, sensitive, and easily angered. They often feel as if they have a chip on their shoulder and could explode at any moment.

This is because criminal thrill seeking has become a central focus in their lives. It has also become a major tool for managing stress and dealing with feelings. When criminal behaviors are taken away, offenders often don't have other ways to manage stress and feel good. As a result, they often become anxious and depressed, feeling trapped and deprived.

**Resolve crisis:** Once the withdrawal symptoms are manageable, the offenders can work on resolving the crisis that inevitably follows them into recovery. The uncontrolled use of alcohol, drugs, and criminal behaviors creates many crisis situations at home, with friends, on the job, and with the legal system. These problems have to be addressed and stabilized.

It is important, however, to keep the addiction and criminal focus. These crisis situations are caused by chemical dependency and criminal personality traits. If the problems are to be resolved, offenders must recognize and accept that they have both of these disorders and not spend so much time dealing with the crisis that they avoid looking at their addiction and criminal personality traits and behaviors. To simply deal with the immediate problem without addressing the two core issues of chemical dependency and criminal personality that caused the problems will result in failure. The person will rapidly relapse into the use of alcohol, drugs, and criminal behaviors.

**Breaking addictive and criminal preoccupation:** Offenders are usually preoccupied with thoughts of drinking, drugging, and criminal thrill seeking. This means that they spend a lot of time thinking about these things when it would be better or more productive for them to think about something else, such as how to recover. They are preoccupied with thoughts of how good it used to be to act out in these old ways, how deprived they are because they cannot act out anymore,

81

and how wonderful it would be if they could once again become a social drinker and recreational drug user who could commit the perfect crime and get away with it. This leads to obsession, compulsion, and craving.

This addictive and criminal preoccupation has to be broken by teaching the offender how to think about other things. Euphoric recalls have to be discussed and the negative aspects of the memories pointed out. The tendency to awfulize recovery has to be stopped by challenging the person to look at the good things that are going on. The magical thinking has to be challenged. Alcohol and drug use won't fix anything. It will just make the offender high, lower the impulse control, and cause him or her to act out in stupid and dangerous ways. Drinking, drugging, and criminal behaviors won't fix anything. They will only result in getting arrested again and going to jail.

**Managing stress:** When the addictive preoccupation is broken it must be replaced by something. This is where stress management comes in. Offenders must learn to cope with life without using alcohol, drugs, and criminal behaviors. Basic stress management procedures are taught. Offenders learn how to do deep breathing, progressive muscle relaxation, meditation, and recreational activities to replace their old coping strategies. They are also taught to redirect their high sensation-seeking tendencies into socially conforming ways. They are taught, for example, to sponsor people in AA and chair meetings instead of running with the old gang.

**Developing hope and motivation:** Chemically dependent offenders begin to develop a sense of hope and motivation as they see their problems settle down. They begin to feel better and are able to cope with life in a positive way. They become motivated to move ahead in their recovery. A vital component in developing hope and motivation is meeting and talking to other people who are successfully recovering from chemical dependency and criminal personality traits.

**The relapse process during stabilization:** During stabilization, chemically dependent criminal offenders tend to experience a classic pattern of relapse warning signs. First they experience *confusion and overreaction*. They find that they can't think or manage feelings, become confused, and have difficulty figuring things out. One moment they are emotionally numb and are unable to feel anything. The next they are emotionally overreactive and feeling overwhelmed by intense emotion.

Then they experience *poor management of situation*. Because they can't think clearly or manage their feelings they begin making mistakes they normally would not make. Their impaired thinking and volatile emotions make it difficult or impossible to cope with these problems effectively.

This leads to *progressive life problems*. One thing leads to another as a viscious self-defeating cycle begins to develop. They can't manage their thoughts and feelings so they do dumb things that cause new problems. The new problems cause more stress, and they get more confused and overreactive. They mismanage the new problems which raises their stress even further and the cycle continues.

This sets up *stress cycles*. The problems become so severe that they are under constant and debilitating stress. They can't calm down or relax. Unable to sleep restfully, they eventually become exhausted and feel like they are going to fall apart.

This leads to *self-condemnation*. The offenders get down on themselves, become critical, and judge themselves harshly. They start to think that they are crazy. This sets them up for a *return of denial*. Once this happens, they experience all of the warning signs that were described as occurring during the transition stage. If the person can overcome these warning signs and complete the tasks of transition, he or she moves into early recovery.

## Stage 3: Early Recovery

During early recovery, offenders learn how to change their addictive and criminal thinking, manage their feelings and emotions in sober and responsible ways, and interrupt their habitual alcohol, drug, and crime-seeking behaviors.

Early recovery consists of four basic tasks: (1) understanding that chemical dependency and criminal personality disorders are treatable diseases; (2) recognizing and accepting that they have these diseases and need to recover; (3) developing sober and responsible ways of thinking, feeling, and acting; and (4) developing a sober and responsible value system. Let's look at these in more detail.

---

### Tasks of Early Recovery

1. Understanding that chemical dependency and criminal personality disorders are treatable diseases
2. Recognizing and accepting that they have these diseases and need to recover
3. Developing sober and responsible ways of thinking, feeling, and acting
4. Developing a sober and responsible value system

---

**Understanding that chemical dependency and criminal personality disorders are treatable diseases:** Long-term recovery begins with an understanding of what chemical dependency and criminal personality traits are and how they operate within a person to cause problems. This task of understanding is a difficult one because most chemically dependent offenders are in denial. They either cannot or will not accept that their alcohol and drug use and their use of antisocial and criminal behaviors are a problem.

To break this denial, recovering offenders must learn the facts about chemical dependency and criminal personality traits. Recovery must be based on a solid foundation of accurate information about the disease progression, the recovery process, the relapse process, and how to access recovery resources. This means education. The offenders must be told about the dynamics of both disorders and have an opportunity to discuss how this information applies to them.

**Recognizing that they have chemical dependency and criminal personality traits and need to recover:** Once recovering offenders understand the basic dynamics of chemical dependency and criminal personality, they need to recognize and accept that they have these conditions. *Recognition* is a cognitive process. It happens in the head when offenders come to see that they are chemically dependent and have criminal personality traits. Recognition occurs as a result of applying the information about these disorders to themselves. *Acceptance* is an emotional process. It happens in the gut as offenders experience the emotional impact of recognizing that they have two serious illnesses.

Recognition develops as offenders complete a series of structured self-assessment exercises. First, they describe their general life history. Next, they review their life history and describe what their alcohol and drug use were like at each stage of their life. Then they describe what the criminal thoughts and behaviors were like at each stage of their life. Finally, they are given self-assessment questionnaires that ask them to assess which symptoms of chemical dependency and criminal personality they have experienced.

Acceptance develops as offenders begin to deal with the feelings and emotions that erupt as they recognize the seriousness of their problems. Most offenders move through a five-stage acceptance process that can be easily remembered by the acronym DABDA, which stands for Denial, Anger, Bargaining, Depression, and Acceptance. At first recovering offenders *deny* they have chemical dependency or criminal personality traits even though there is plenty of evidence in their histories and questionnaires to prove that they do. Next they get *angry* and try to threaten or intimidate their way out of the diagnosis. They use their anger to provoke situations that take the focus off their chemical dependency and criminal personality traits.

Then they begin to *bargain*: "Maybe I'm a little bit chemically dependent and have a few criminal personality traits, but it's not that bad. I'll just cut back and control it." Then, as the reality of their condition begins to sink in, they become depressed. They often sink into a "zero state" where they believe they are nothing and will never amount to anything. With proper counseling they can move out of this zero state and into a deep state of acceptance. With *acceptance* they know they are chemically dependent and have criminal personality traits, but they also know they can change. They become motivated to recover and begin to see that this new knowledge about themselves, as painful as it might be, represents the first step of getting free from these two crippling diseases.

**Developing sober and responsible ways of thinking, feeling, and acting:** With recognition and acceptance comes the responsibility to change. It is not enough to say, "I have these diseases!" Recovering offenders must go the next step and make a decision to change.

First they must change how they think. Chemically dependent offenders have three voices talking with them all the time. Two of these voices are very loud and encourage them to relapse. The other is usually very quiet and prompts them to recover. The first voice is the *addictive self* that tells offenders they have a right to use alcohol and drugs, that anyone who tries to take away that right is an enemy, and that they can handle alcohol and drug use.

The second voice is the *criminal self*, which tells offenders they have a right to get what they want when they want and that no one has a right to stop them. The criminal self challenges authority and tries to persuade offenders they are all-powerful and god-like. This voice says, "You have a right to have it your way and no one has a right to stop you! Responsible living is for chumps. You're smarter than to be chump!"

The third—and usually the quietest voice—is that of the *sober and responsible self* that affirms the reality that they do suffer from both chemical dependency and criminal personality traits. The sober self argues that it is good to know about chemical dependency and criminal personality traits because this knowledge provides the opportunity to change. The sober and responsible self recognizes that, in the long run, sober and responsible living will pay off while addictive and criminal living will destroy their lives.

Recovering offenders must learn to identify the thoughts, feelings, and action urges associated with each of these three voices. They must learn to identify and successfully challenge the addictive and criminal voices that argue in their heads. They must learn to recognize and support the sober voice.

**Developing a sober and responsible value system:** A value is something that people are willing to invest time, energy, and resources to acquire and maintain. People with *sober value systems* are willing to invest time, energy, and resources to learn how to get sober and stay that way. People with *responsible value systems* are willing to invest time, energy, and resources in learning how to be accountable and responsible.

The bottom line is this: Long-term recovery is only possible if offenders learn how to value sobriety and responsibility above everything else. They must be willing to invest in their recovery program. They must also challenge old addictive and criminal values that told them it is worth investing in alcohol, drugs, and criminal behaviors.

**The relapse process during early recovery:** During early recovery, chemically dependent offenders tend to experience a classic pattern of relapse warning signs. First they experience the zero state: "I am nothing, I will never be anything, and everyone knows it." This leads to *addictive and criminal thinking* and *emotional mismanagement*. They start to use old patterns of addictive and criminal thinking to restore self-esteem and give them the illusion that they are back in control. They also begin to mismanage their feelings in one of two ways. At times they stuff their feelings, build up like a pressure cooker, overreact, act out in self-defeating ways, and later feel regret and remorse. This pattern is typical of the addictive self. At other times they exaggerate or intensify their feelings, convert the feelings to anger, act out against others in criminal ways, and then blame the victim to justify what they have done. This pattern is typical of the criminal self. Because most chemically dependent criminal offenders have both disorders, they often vacillate between both styles of emotional mismanagement.

This leads to a *return to an addiction and crime-centered lifestyle*. They begin to hang around with people who are drinking, drugging, and using criminal behaviors. At first they convince themselves they won't do these things—they are just hanging out with friends and being in places where they feel comfortable. Eventually the contact with people, places, and things where they used to drink, drug, and commit crimes reactivates old patterns of thinking and triggers a craving or urge to use alcohol, drugs, and criminal behaviors.

They now get *overwhelmed by pain and problems*. They have broken contact with their support system and are being influenced by people who are still acting out in addictive and criminal ways. As a result, there is no place to go with the pain and the only advice they get for coping with the problems is to use alcohol, drugs, and criminal behaviors to magically fix them. They now *refuse to comply with their recovery program*. They tell themselves they can handle it alone or with their old friends. They stop following a consistent daily structure. Their stress increases and they become confused and overreactive, and all of the warning signs described during the stabilization stage tend to get activated.

## Stage 4: Middle Recovery

During middle recovery, offenders repair past damage caused by the use of alcohol, drugs, and criminal behavior. They learn how to develop a lifestyle that is centered on sobriety and responsibility instead of alcohol, drugs, and crime.

Middle recovery consists of four basic tasks: (1) repair lifestyle damage; (2) adjust their recovery program to deal with lifestyle problems; (3) balance their lifestyle; and (4) learn to manage change. Let's look at these in more detail.

### The Tasks of Middle Recovery
1. Repair lifestyle damage
2. Adjust their recovery program to deal with lifestyle problems
3. Balance their lifestyle
4. Learn to manage change

**Repair lifestyle damage:** Chemical dependency and criminal personality disorders hurt people and damage the lifestyle. Few areas of life are unaffected. Relationships with lovers, family members, friends, employers, coworkers, and acquaintances are seriously affected. In order to recover, the damage that was done to these relationships needs to be repaired.

Recovering offenders are asked to make a list of all the people who were hurt by their use of alcohol, drugs, or criminal behaviors and describe what they did that hurt each person. Then they are asked to set up a plan for what they can do to repair the damage. If they stole something, they pay it back. If they broke something, they fix it or replace it. If they hurt others, they make honest amends and assume responsibility for what they did and its consequences. Then they are asked to systematically do what needs to be done with each significant person in their life to repair the damage. This process is often called *making amends*.

**Adjust their recovery program to deal with lifestyle problems:** To make amends, recovering offenders may have to adjust their recovery program. To repair the damage done to their marriage, they may need to go to marriage counseling. To repair the damage done to their relationship with their children they may need professional help in addition to regularly scheduled time with their children. To repair their career they may need job retraining or career counseling. So at this point, offenders begin to build a bridge from the rigidly structured recovery program that they used in stabilization and early recovery to a more flexible recovery program designed to meet their individual needs in building a balanced lifestyle.

**Balance their lifestyle:** Once they have repaired the damage from the past, the next job is to establish a balanced lifestyle. To be happy and functional most people find that they have to balance their time among four basic areas: physical health, psychological health, social health, and spiritual health. Each area requires time and energy. *Physical health* requires attention to proper diet, regular exercise, stress management, and basic health management. *Psychological health* requires a commitment to learn how to think clearly, logically, and rationally; how to recognize, label, and communicate feelings and emotions honestly; and how to behave responsibly by thinking before acting and evaluating after acting. *Social health* means building a healthy social network that consists of acquaintances, companions, friends, intimate partners, and family members. *Spiritual health* involves connecting with a sense of meaning and purpose in life. It also means reconnecting with the conscious voice within that gives a sense of inner stability and gauge for measuring right and wrong. Now a person has the foundation necessary to manage the ups and downs of life.

**Learn to manage change:** Sometimes it seems like the only constant in life is change. As soon as we become comfortable and competent in one situation, things change and we are thrust into new situations. The most valuable skill learned in middle recovery is the ability to roll with the punches and get back up after being knocked down. The more successful the recovering person is at managing change while maintaining a good sense of self-esteem and a healthy respect for other people, the more likely it is that he or she will make a full recovery.

**The relapse process during middle recovery:** During middle recovery, chemically dependent offenders tend to experience a classic pattern of relapse warning signs. First they *fail to repair lifestyle damage caused by their addiction and criminality*. Sometimes they remain in denial that these problems exist. At other times they know that they have these problems but either refuse to or are unable to face them directly and resolve them.

Then the *unresolved problems affect recovery*. They begin to feel they are stuck and cannot move on. They feel as if they are not making any progress and don't know why. This creates a state of *chronic, low-grade emergency*, which leaves them feeling uncomfortable almost all the time. They appear to lose the capacity to enjoy life and rarely, if ever, feel really good.

This leads them into *circular problem solving*. They discuss their problems over and over again with no resolution. They talk a good game but refuse to take action to directly address the lifestyle problems. As a result they *feel demoralized*: "Nothing will ever get better, so why bother to try!"

This results in a *buildup of stress and pain*. They start to hurt so badly they can't stand it. The pain becomes overwhelming and it appears that nothing they are doing is helping. This is when they *refuse to comply with their recovery program*: "Since my recovery program isn't working for me, why should I keep doing these things?" At this point they become confused, experience debilitating stress, and begin experiencing the relapse warning signs described in the stabilization section.

## Stage 5: Late Recovery

During late recovery, offenders learn how to make deep changes in their personality and value systems by exploring their family of origin and recognizing the types of changes in basic beliefs and values that they need to make to live meaningful and comfortable lives without alcohol, drugs, or criminal thrill seeking.

Chemically dependent offenders should not be thrust into late recovery too soon because they have a tendency to blame current behaviors on their childhood experiences, their parents, or society in general. They must learn to deal with their lives in sober, responsible ways in the here-and-now regardless of what happened in their past. Once they have a stable support system in place, then they can do in-depth work on understanding and changing core values and personality traits.

Late recovery consists of five basic tasks: (1) recognizing

current personality problems; (2) linking current problems to training in their family of origin; (3) examining their childhood to identify values, attitudes, and coping styles; (4) applying this knowledge to current problems; and (5) changing personality traits and lifestyle patterns. Let's look at these in more detail.

---

### The Tasks of Late Recovery

1. Recognizing current personality problems
2. Linking current problems to training in their family of origin
3. Examining childhood to identify values, attitudes, and coping styles
4. Applying this knowledge to current problems
5. Changing personality traits and lifestyle patterns

---

**Recognizing current personality problems:** In late recovery, chemically dependent offenders have recognized that they have chemical dependency and criminal personality traits. They have stabilized their immediate crisis and motivating problems that forced them into treatment. They have also changed their old patterns of addictive and criminal thinking, feeling, and acting, and have developed a solid and balanced social life. Despite these changes they don't feel at peace. There is a nagging feeling that something is wrong, and they are constantly battling an urge or tendency to set themselves up to fail.

The problem is that they are fighting against the urge to act out old self-defeating personality traits. They have changed behaviors and lifestyles without clearly identifying and changing their underlying values, attitudes, and core beliefs that motivate them to act out the old self-defeating behaviors and lifestyle preferences. As a result, despite their progress in recovery, they periodically tend to feel frustrated, unhappy, and deprived without understanding why.

They can clearly see that the old lifestyle centered on alcohol, drugs, and criminal behaviors doesn't work anymore, and they really don't want to live that way anymore. They also realize their new lifestyle causes fewer problems and provides more opportunities than their old one. Yet something is missing. There is an emptiness inside. They feel trapped in a void between two very different ways of life. The sick romanticizing of the criminal and addictive lifestyle doesn't work anymore, yet they cannot find the thrills and excitement they crave within the confines of sober and responsible living. The solution is to find out where this need for self-defeating thrill seeking through the use of alcohol, drugs, and criminal behavior comes from.

**Link current problems to training in their family of origin:** Like it or not we are all affected by our family of origin, and recovering offenders are no exception. At the time of conception we genetically inherit a set of temperaments that create preferences for certain ways of thinking, feeling, and acting. These genetic temperaments interact with our early childhood experiences to create our first or primal personality. We develop an initial and intuitive sense of who we are, who other people are, and how we should relate to them. We also develop a sense of what the world is all about and what we must do to survive in it.

As result of this intuitive learning, we develop deeply entrenched ways of thinking, feeling, and acting that allow us to survive in the world as we experience it and believe it to be. In essence, every child creates within his or her mind the "truth as I see it" about the world, others, and themselves. This concept of truth is based on early childhood experience. It is not logically constructed. It emerges in a nonrational way from our early childhood experiences.

To fully recover, to learn how to completely surrender the old way of life, recovering offenders need to examine the roots of their criminal and addictive urges and trace them back to the childhood patterns that shaped them. This knowledge will give the basis of true freedom to "invent" a life based on their currently healthy needs. The old adage is true, "The truth shall set you free!" The problem is that it usually makes you miserable before you get free. This is because you have to look at the painful unfinished experiences of childhood and understand how they are shaping your current approach to life in order to find that freedom.

**Examining their childhood to identify values, attitudes, and coping styles:** Late recovery revolves around the central task of exploring how childhood patterns are affecting choices and reactions in life right now. This examination of childhood is detailed and specific, but it is also focused on here-and-now problems. The key questions are: How am I acting out childhood patterns now? How is unfinished business from my childhood making me unhappy and limiting my potential in the here and now? These questions are answered by following a standard process.

First, recovering offenders must clearly identify the problems and self-defeating urges they are struggling with in their current recovery. These need to be written down and organized. Many offenders find it is helpful to write three problem statements. The first begins, "My current beliefs about who I am and how I should act in life that are causing me pain and problems are...." The second statement begins, "My current beliefs about other people that are causing me pain and problems are...." The third statement begins, "My current beliefs about the world in general that are causing me pain and problems are...."

Next they must write the detailed story of their childhood. This normally involves describing in detail how they, as very young children, remember their mother, father, brothers, and sisters. They also describe the important events or experiences that shaped their early lives. The goal is to look for a general pattern of responses or coping skills that became deeply entrenched in the personality. Most people adapt to childhood problems in one of three ways. They become a top dog, an underdog, or a coequal player.

*Top dogs* learn to cope with life by acting bigger, meaner, and stronger than everyone else. They put themselves in a one-up position, threatening and intimidating others into a one-down position. Privately they feel inadequate and insecure. As a result life is a constant power struggle. They must always prove themselves better than others and judge other people and put them down. Top dogs mistakenly believe that if they are ever viewed as equal to or less than others something awful will happen. Top dogs are often described as being extremely independent or counterdependent.

*Underdogs* learn to cope with life by acting weaker and less adequate than every else. They put themselves in a one-down position and perceive others as being more powerful. They believe that other people should take care of them and rescue them from the problems of life. When other people don't do this, they get angry, resentful, and quietly judgmental. They manipulate in underground ways because they believe they could never win in a direct, open conflict. Underdogs are often described as being extremely dependent or codependent.

*Coequal players* see themselves as being equal to others. They do not believe they are inherently better than others or worse than others. As a result they do not try to control or manipulate others but negotiate as an equal. They recognize they have both strengths and weaknesses. They can act on their strengths openly and directly, and they can also ask for help in dealing with their weaknesses without feeling shame or guilt.

**Applying this knowledge to current problems:** The goal in late recovery is for recovering offenders to identify whether they learned to cope as a child by becoming a top dog or an underdog. They must then see how they have continued to act out that style of coping throughout their lives. They must learn to recognize the patterns of thinking, feeling, and acting that go along with their childhood coping style. They must learn how to shift from a top dog or underdog position, how to perceive themselves, and to start thinking, feeling, and acting like a coequal player.

**Change lifestyle:** The final task that recovering offenders have to complete in late recovery is changing their lifestyle. As their self-concept changes from that of a top dog who has a right to abuse or control others, or that of an underdog who has no choice but to be victimized by others, they begin to see their lives differently. They can see how they have set up their lifestyle to support their old concept of self and their old style of coping with life. As they begin to change, they must renegotiate relationships, perhaps change jobs, and begin setting a lifestyle that supports the image of a coequal player who treats others fairly and expects to be treated fairly in return.

**The relapse process during late recovery:** The major cause of relapse during the late recovery stage is pain from unresolved family-of-origin issues that creates constant pain and problems in recovery. The typical warning signs progress like this. First they experience *inner pain*. This is usually caused by the unresolved symptoms of post traumatic stress disorder (PTSD) or other mental disorders that are triggered by the new, more advanced recovery tasks. At other times, the dissatisfaction is related to the slow buildup of stress and pressure that results from the use of the rigid, self-defeating personality traits associated with the top dog and underdog styles previously described. (These self-defeating personality traits are often called character defects in Twelve Step programs.)

Instead of identifying and dealing directly with these personality problems, recovering offenders *seek external sources of relief.* They want someone or something else to fix them. This leads them into a *dysfunctional lifestyle.* They start developing new problems in recovery and mismanage those problems. This leads to *dissatisfaction and despair.* They begin to feel there is no way out. Their lives become progressively more unmanageable, and they begin to experience the relapse warning signs described under middle recovery.

## Stage 6: Maintenance

During maintenance offenders maintain a program of continuing growth and development, guard against relapse, and deal responsibly with problems as they arise.

Maintenance consists of four basic tasks: (1) maintaining a recovery program; (2) practicing daily coping; (3) continuing to grow and develop as a person; and (4) coping with life transitions. Let's look at these in more detail.

---

### The Tasks of Maintenance
1. Maintaining a recovery program
2. Practicing daily coping
3. Continuing to grow and develop as a person
4. Coping with life transitions

---

**Maintaining a recovery program:** The first job of maintenance is to maintain a recovery program. Chemical dependency and criminal personality disorder go into remission but they are never fully cured. As soon as recovering offenders stop actively working a recovery program, they are at risk of falling back into old ways of thinking, feeling, acting, and living that can lead them back into the use of alcohol, drugs, and criminal behaviors.

**Practicing daily coping:** Recovery doesn't mean having a problem-free life. All people, even those in solid recovery, experience problems. Recovery means being able to cope with and resolve problems without having to resort to the use of alcohol, drugs, or criminal behaviors. This means that to stay in recovery, people must become skilled at recognizing and solving problems promptly as they occur.

**Continuing to grow and develop as a person:** Maintenance is an active process of growth and development. People learn, grow, and change constantly throughout the life cycle. The first step toward relapse is to become rigid and to stop the process of change. To stay in recovery means keeping centered, being aware of changes and opportunities to grow, and taking advantage of those opportunities.

**Coping with life transitions:** One of the frustrating things about life is that it constantly changes. As soon as we get comfortable being a child we move into adolescence. Once we master life as a teenager we become a young adult and so on. Every time we get competent at one stage of life we are propelled into the next stage and we typically feel unprepared. In maintenance, recovering people learn about normal adult development and how to anticipate and deal with these normal life transitions.

**The relapse process during maintenance:** The major cause of relapse during maintenance is a sense of complacency that causes offenders to neglect their recovery. The feeling is, "I've come this far, I have it made! Why should I have to keep putting so much energy into my recovery program?" Things go well until they hit a problem or crisis and then they get overwhelmed. The process unfolds like this:

Offenders become *overconfident and complacent*. They believe they are cured and that nothing could possibly go

99

wrong that would get them in trouble. Because of this they *stop working at personal growth*. They feel they have done everything they need to do and therefore don't need to keep learning or growing. Once they stop growing, it is easy to get back into a *self-centered lifestyle*. They decide that they will think of themselves and not worry so much about other people. They deserve it, they believe, because they have worked so hard at their recovery program and they have come so far.

Now they are vulnerable. They experience a *life crisis or life transition*. These new problems overwhelm them and they find they are *unable to cope or ask for help*. They try to tough it out by themselves but things keep getting worse until *severe lifestyle problems develop* and they begin to experience all of the warning signs described in middle recovery.

## Stuck Points in Recovery

Although some recovering offenders progress through the stages of recovery without complications, the majority do not. They typically get stuck somewhere midstream. They hit a point where they either cannot or will not move ahead in their recovery.

Recovering people tend to get stuck for one of three reasons: They can't, they won't, or they don't know how to move ahead in recovery. When people *can't* move ahead by completing the next recovery task, it is usually because they perceive the task as being too difficult. They feel overwhelmed or too frightened to try. When they *won't* move ahead, it is because they refuse to try. They don't want to invest the time, energy, or resources necessary to complete the task at hand. When people *don't know how* to move ahead in recovery, they generally lack knowledge and skills. They don't know what they are supposed to do or they don't know how to do it. They need education and skill training.

It is important to tell recovering offenders that it is normal and natural to periodically get stuck in recovery. It happens to everyone and doesn't mean they are going to relapse. It is how offenders cope with the stuck points that determine whether they move ahead in recovery or begin to move toward relapse. It is their responsibility to understand the common stuck points and the constructive and self-defeating ways of coping with them. It is ultimately their responsibility to learn how to get the help they need to deal with each stuck point and to move ahead in their recovery process. They must understand the relapse prone coping style and how to interrupt it *and* the recovery prone style and how to reinforce it.

The relapse prone coping style can best be described by using the acronym ESCAPE. They *evade and deny* the stuck point: "I'm not stuck! There is nothing wrong with me! Who says that you have to do this to recover anyway? I'm fine the way I am?" This denial and evasion causes *stress*. It takes energy to deny reality and to manipulate around problems without directly acknowledging them. As the stress builds up, recovering offenders start using *compulsive behaviors* to cope with the stress. They start to overwork, overeat, gamble, or act out sexually. They feel a strong urge to do anything to get their minds off their problems and make the stress go away. The compulsive behavior leads to *avoidance of others*. They begin to isolate and spend more time alone in an effort to lower their stress levels. The evasion and denial, growing stress levels, compulsive behaviors, and isolation begin to cause new *problems*. These problems are once again dealt with by *evasion, denial, and recycling*. They keep repeating this self-destructive cycle until serious relapse warning signs begin to develop.

## The Developmental Model of Recovery
## For the Chemically Dependent Criminal Offender
Developed by Terence T. Gorski (Copyright T. Gorski 1993, All Rights Reserved)

| Transition | Stabilization | Early Recovery | Middle Recovery | Late Recovery | Maintenance |
|---|---|---|---|---|---|
| 1. Developing motivating problems | 1. Using a structured recovery program | 1. Understanding that CD criminal personality disorders are treatable diseases | 1. Repairing life-style damage | 1. Recognizing current personality problems | 1. Maintaining a recovery program |
| 2. Attempting normal problem solving | 2. Stabilizing crisis | 2. Recognizing and accepting that they have these diseases and need to recover | 2. Adjusting their recovery program to deal with lifestyle problems | 2. Linking current problems to training in their family of origin | 2. Practicing daily coping |
| 3. Attempting to cut back or control | 3. Breaking addictive and criminal preoccupation | 3. Developing sober and responsible ways of thinking, feeling, and acting | 3. Balancing their lifestyle | 3. Examining their childhood to identify values, attitudes, and coping styles | 3. Continuing to grow and develop as a person |
| 4. Attempting to stop without help | 4. Managing stress | 4. Developing a sober and responsible value system | 4. Learning to manage change | 4. Applying this knowledge to current problems | 4. Coping with life transitions |
| 5. Accepting help | 5. Developing hope and motivation | | | 5. Changing personality and lifestyle patterns | |

Reprinted from *A Professional Guide to Relapse Prevention Therapy with Chemically Dependent Criminal Offender* (Herald House/Independence Press)

## Relapse Prone Coping Style—ESCAPE

E = Evade and Deny
S = Stress
C = Compulsive Behavior
A = Avoidance
P = Problems
E = Evade, Deny, and Recycle

The recovery prone coping style can be described by using the acronym RADAR. When people get stuck, they *recognize* they are stuck. They acknowledge the stuck point by saying things to themselves like, "I'm stuck in my recovery. I have a problem that I need to cope with. If I recognize this now and cope with it I can handle it before it gets out of control."

They can then *accept* that it is okay to have the problem and to get stuck. They tell themselves, "It is normal and natural to get stuck. Everyone gets stuck from time to time and I am no exception. I have nothing to be ashamed of. It is how I deal with this stuck point that will determine whether I get back on track in recovery or begin to fall apart and move toward relapse."

This allows them to *detach* from the problem. They say to themselves, "I don't have to deal with this problem right now all by myself." They learn they can temporarily turn the problem over. They can avoid a sudden, knee-jerk reaction and think the problem and its solution through before they act.

This gives them time and motivation to *ask for help*. They ask the advice of people who have experience in dealing with the problems they are currently experiencing. They can also take time for meditation and contemplation so they can find a source of courage and hope that gives them the strength to do what needs to be done to manage the problem. As a result they can *respond with action*. They can do what needs to be done to resolve the problem and to move ahead in recovery.

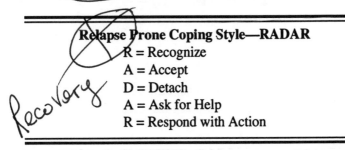

**Relapse Prone Coping Style—RADAR**
R = Recognize
A = Accept
D = Detach
A = Ask for Help
R = Respond with Action

If recovering offenders use this relapse prone style, they will be able to deal effectively with the stuck point and move on to the next proactive step of the DMR. If they don't, they usually begin to experience progressively more severe problems in sobriety. They start to fall apart and experience a progression of predictable relapse warning signs that lead from stable recovery back to the use of alcohol, drugs, and criminal behaviors.

# Chapter 4

# Relapse Warning Signs

Relapse is a process that begins long before chemically dependent offenders begin to use alcohol, drugs, or criminal behaviors. The relapse process begins when recovering offenders start mismanaging problems and, as a result, feel progressive pain and discomfort in sobriety. This pain and discomfort can become so severe that they cannot live normally in recovery. In AA this is called a "dry drunk." Other people call it "building up to drink" (BUD). Recovering people can start hurting so badly that they convince themselves that chemical use can't be any worse than the pain of staying sober.

Relapse is not the isolated event of using alcohol, drugs, and criminal behavior. There are predictable and observable warning signs that occur before recovering offenders return to the use. This means that recovering offenders can learn to avoid relapse by recognizing and managing critical relapse warning signs.

Relapse warning signs are a lot like fingerprints. Everybody has them, but each person's fingerprints are unique. All recovering offenders will experience a similar progression of thoughts, feelings, and behaviors that lead them from stable recovery to relapse. Each recovering person, however, will have unique differences in the type of warning signs that are experienced and the order or sequence in which they occur.

When relapse prone offenders are first introduced to the relapse warning signs for chemical dependency and criminal behavior, they are often surprised. These lists accurately describe experiences they have had and have kept secret or have never been able to describe in words. They feel like someone has been reading their mail.

A good relapse warning sign list describes the progression from stable recovery to the use of alcohol, drugs, and criminal behaviors in a way that is simple and easy to understand. The warning signs accurately reflect the experiences of the relapse prone client so he or she is able to quickly identify with the warning signs and relate to them.

This chapter will explain the concept of relapse warning signs in a way that is easy for chemically dependent criminal offenders and their families to understand. The goal in explaining the warning signs is to give offenders words to describe their own relapse warning signs. For relapse warning signs to be an effective tool in preventing relapse, offenders must develop a personalized warning sign list in their own words. They must describe their own personal process of moving from stable recovery back to the use of alcohol, drugs, and criminal behavior. The more personalized the list the more effective it will be in helping offenders identify and manage warning signs before they relapse.

I will explain four brief models for understanding relapse warning signs and then present two comprehensive warning sign lists. The first comprehensive list describes the typical warning signs that occur before a chemically dependent person starts using alcohol and drugs. The second comprehensive list describes the warning signs that occur before an habitual criminal offender returns to the use of criminal behaviors.

## Brief Warning Sign Models

It is important to have several different models for understanding relapse warning signs. Brief models will allow you to briefly explain the concept of relapse warning signs to offenders quickly and easily. There are four brief warning sign models: (1) the Attitude Change Model, (2) the Progressive Dysfunction Model, (3) the Stress Model, and (4) the Craving Model. Each of these models can be explained in three or four minutes. Each describes a different pathway to relapse.

### Brief Warning Sign Models

| Attitude Change | Progressive Dysfunction | Stress | Craving |
|---|---|---|---|
| 1. Change in attitude | 1. Internal change | 1. Stress | 1. Trigger event |
| 2. Change in behavior | 2. External change | 2. Unmanageable thoughts and feelings | 2. Obsession, compulsion, and craving |
| 3. Change in situation | 3. Progressive life problems | 3. Self-defeating behavior | 3. Drug-seeking behavior |
| 4. Use of alcohol, drugs, and criminal behavior | 4. Use of alcohol, drugs, and criminal behavior | 4. Use of alcohol drugs, and criminal behavior | 4. Use of alcohol drugs, and criminal behavior |

**The Attitude Change Model of Relapse:** For some people the pathway to relapse begins with a *change in attitude*. Recovery is no longer a priority. They begin to believe that other things are more important than staying away from alcohol, drugs, and criminal behavior.

This leads them into a *change in behavior*. Their old ways of behaving return. They start acting differently when they attend group therapy, individual therapy, or Twelve Step meetings. They bring the body to these meetings, but the way they think and manage their feelings is different. They become overconfident and believe they are cured. They believe other things are more important than their recovery and start to act that way.

This leads to a *change in situation*. They put themselves around people, places, and things that support alcohol, drugs, and criminal behaviors. They start avoiding people who put recovery as a number one priority. They start to come late for sessions or miss them altogether. They generally have a good excuse—something more important is always coming up. Once they have stopped their recovery program and put themselves back into old situations, it is just a matter of time until they start the *use of alcohol, drugs, and criminal behavior*.

**The Progressive Dysfunction Model of Relapse:** For other people the process begins with *internal change*. Addictive thinking and feelings return. Addictive thinking is based on protecting the right to use alcohol, drugs, and criminal behavior. The person feels deprived because he or she can't use anymore and starts romanticizing the old way of living by thinking how great or wonderful it was. Addictive feelings center around obsession, compulsion, and craving. The person slowly develops a desire to start using again.

This leads to *external change*. The person begins using irresponsible or self-defeating behaviors to cope with life problems. Instead of planning before they do something and evaluating when they are done to see if it worked, recovering offenders begin to act impulsively without thought. They stop thinking about what they did and how well it worked. Instead of taking personal responsibility when things go wrong, they begin to blame others.

This leads to *progressive life problems*. They start to become overwhelmed by problems in recovery. Nothing they do works, and the harder they try, the worse their problems seem to get. Eventually things get so bad they believe they must return to the *use of alcohol, drugs, and criminal behaviors* to deal with their problems.

**The Stress Model of Relapse:** Another pathway to relapse begins with *stress*. The stress is usually caused by change. Something happens that forces the person to do things or become involved in situations that makes him or her feel uncomfortable.

The stress and change trigger *unmanageable thoughts and feelings*. The mind begins to race and old ways of thinking come back. They begin to either stuff or overreact to their feelings and emotions. They can't get their mind to shut down or their feelings to calm down.

This leads to *self-defeating behavior*. They begin mismanaging their problems, and things keep getting worse until they feel overwhelmed by life in recovery. "If this is recovery," they think to themselves, "who needs it?" With this attitude it is just a matter of time until they return to the *use of alcohol, drugs, and criminal behavior.*

**The Craving Model of Relapse:** Another pathway to relapse is quite common for people addicted to cocaine and other stimulant drugs. For many of these people the relapse process begins with a *trigger event*. It can be an internal thought, feeling, or memory or something external that is seen, heard, touched, or tasted. These trigger events usually remind recovering people of the feelings they experienced while getting high. The trigger event automatically activates *obsession* (out-of-control thinking about use), *compulsion* (an irrational urge to use), and *craving* (a body hunger for the drugs). Once the trigger activates obsession, compulsion, and craving, recovering people move into automatic drug-seeking behavior. They begin putting themselves around old people, places, and things associated with chemical use and criminal behaviors. This makes the craving worse, they lose control, and start the *use of alcohol, drugs, and criminal behavior.*

## The Need to Personalize

As can be seen by these brief warning sign models, the process of relapsing usually begins with the recovering person being in a stable recovery. There are six criteria used to determine when offenders are in stable recovery: (1) they are abstinent from alcohol, drugs, and criminal behaviors; (2) they are free from cravings or urges to use alcohol, drugs, and criminal behaviors; (3) they are actively following a structured recovery program; (4) their recovery program has become an habitual part of their life and they no longer feel resistance or an urge to stop participating; (5) they are actively working on completing recovery tasks appropriate to their current stage of recovery; and (6) they are currently not experiencing any physical, psychological, or social crisis or problem that is threatening their abstinence or their continued involvement in their recovery program.

Recovering offenders then move through a series of predictable warning signs that make their lives progressively more unmanageable. As the problems in their lives become more severe, they begin to think about using alcohol, drugs, and criminal behaviors. These thoughts activate obsessions and compulsion, and this leads to loss of control. The process ends with a renewed use of alcohol, drugs, and criminal behavior.

Notice, however, that each of these brief models describes this process in a slightly different way. It is important to be able to explain relapse warning signs in a way that relates to the experience of the individual recovering offender that you are working with. The main goal is to personalize the relapse warning signs.

With that in mind, let's look at two comprehensive lists of warning signs. The first is **Relapse Warning Signs for Chemical Dependency**. These warning signs were developed by interviewing relapse prone chemically dependent people who did not have criminal personality traits. The second list is **Relapse Warning Signs for Criminal Offenders**. These warning signs were developed based on experiences with chemically dependent criminal offenders who had criminal personality traits.

Both of these warning signs are written in the first person. As you read the lists, attempt to put yourself in the position of a recovering chemically dependent criminal offender. See if you can get inside of their skin and experience what it is like to try to live a sober, responsible life only to find that things keep falling apart and that nothing you do in recovery appears to work.

## Relapse Warning Signs for Chemical Dependency

This relapse warning sign list was originally developed in 1973 after analyzing the relapse histories of 118 relapse prone alcoholic patients. These alcoholics had four things in common: they had completed a twenty-one or twenty-eight-day rehabilitation program for alcoholism; they had recognized that they were alcoholics and could not safely use alcohol or other drugs; when they left rehabilitation they had the conscious intention of staying permanently sober by using both Alcoholics Anonymous (AA) and professional counseling; and they eventually returned to the addictive use of alcohol and drugs despite their initial commitment to remain sober.

After more than twenty years of use in a variety of treatment settings, counselors and recovering people still find this list of warning signs to be a useful tool in identifying and managing the typical problems that lead recovering people from stable recovery to relapse.

**Phase 1: Internal Change:** During this phase I look good on the outside, but I start using old addictive ways of thinking and managing feelings that make me feel bad on the inside. The most common relapse warning signs are:

111

1-1. *Increased Stress:* I begin to feel more stressed than usual. Sometimes this is the result of a problem or situation that is easy to see. At other times it is the result of little problems that cause stress to build up slowly over time.

1-2. *Change in Thinking:* I begin to think that my recovery program is not as important as it used to be. Sometimes things are going so well that I don't believe that I need to put a lot of effort into my program. At other times I have problems that my recovery program doesn't seem to help and I ask myself, "Why bother?"

1-3. *Change in Feeling:* I start having unpleasant feelings that I don't like. Sometimes I feel euphoric, like everything is going my way when I know that it really is not. At other times I feel depressed, like nothing is working out. I know that these mood sweeps are not good for me.

1-4. *Change in Behavior:* I start acting different. I still look and sound good on the outside, but I know deep inside that I am not practicing my program the way I used to. Deep inside I know that something is going wrong.

**Phase 2: Denial:** During this phase I stop paying attention to or honestly telling others what I am thinking and feeling. The most common relapse warning signs are:

2-1. *Worrying about Myself:* I feel uneasy about the changes in my thinking, feelings, and behavior. This uneasiness comes and goes and usually lasts only a short time. Sometimes I feel afraid that I won't be able to stay sober, but I don't want to think about it.

2-2. *Denying that I'm Worried:* I deal with this uneasiness in the same way I used to deal with my addiction—I go into denial and try to convince myself that everything is okay when it really isn't. Sometimes the denial works and I can forget my problems and feel better for a little while. I usually don't know that I am using denial when I am doing it. It is only when

I think about the situation later that I am able to recognize how bad I was feeling and how I denied those feelings.

**Phase 3: Avoidance and Defensiveness:** During this phase, I try to avoid anyone or anything that will force me to be honest about how my thinking, feelings, and behavior have changed. If I am directly confronted, I get defensive and can't hear what others are trying to tell me. The most common relapse warning signs are:

3-1. *Believing I'll Never Use Alcohol or Drugs:* I convince myself that I don't need to put a lot of energy into my recovery program today because I will probably never go back to alcohol or drug use. I tend to keep this belief to myself. Sometimes I am afraid to tell my counselor or other recovering people about this belief for fear of being confronted. At other times I think that it is none of their business.

3-2. *Worrying about Others instead of Self:* I take the focus off myself by becoming more concerned about the sobriety of others than about my personal recovery. I privately judge the drinking of my friends and spouse and the recovery programs of other recovering people. I keep these private judgments to myself and don't talk about them. This is often called "working the other guy's program."

3-3. *Defensiveness:* I feel reluctant to discuss personal problems and what I am doing in my recovery because I am afraid I will be criticized or confronted. I feel scared, angry, and defensive when other people ask me questions about my recovery program or point out things about my recovery that I don't want to see. I tend to get defensive even when no defense is necessary.

3-4. *Compulsive Behavior:* I start using compulsive behaviors to keep my mind off how uncomfortable I am feeling. I get stuck in old, rigid, and self-defeating ways of thinking and acting. I tend to do the same things over and over again without a good reason. I try to control conversations either by talking too much or not talking at all. I start working more than I need to and get involved in many activities. Other people think that I am the model of recovery because of my heavy involvement in Twelve Step work and chairing meetings. I become active in my therapy group by "playing therapist" but I am reluctant to talk about my personal problems. I avoid casual or informal involvement with people unless I can be in control.

3-5. *Impulsive Behavior:* I start creating problems for myself by using poor judgment and impulsively doing things without thinking them through. This usually happens at times of high stress. Sometimes I privately feel bad but I tend to make excuses and blame others for the problems.

3-6. *Tendencies toward Loneliness:* I start feeling uncomfortable around others and begin spending more time alone. I usually have good reasons and excuses for staying away from other people. I start feeling lonely. Instead of dealing with the loneliness by trying to meet and be around other people, I get more compulsive about doing things alone.

**Phase 4: Crisis Building:** During this phase I start having problems in sobriety that I don't understand. Even though I want to solve these problems and work hard at it, two new problems pop up to replace every problem that I solve. The most common warning signs are:

4-1. *Tunnel Vision:* I start to think that my life is made up of separate and unrelated parts. I focus on one small part of my life and block out everything else. Sometimes I focus only on the good things and block out or ignore the bad. In this way I can mistakenly believe everything is fine when it really isn't. At other times I see only what is going wrong and blow that out of proportion. This causes me to feel like nothing is going my way even when there are many good things happening in my life. As a result I can't see "the big picture" or figure out how what I do in one part of my life can cause problems in other parts of my life. When problems develop I don't know why. I believe that life is unfair and that I have no power to do anything about it.

4-2. *Minor Depression:* I start to feel depressed, down, blue, listless, and empty of feelings. I lack energy, tend to sleep too much, and rarely feel good or full of life. I am able to distract myself from these moods by getting busy with other things and not talking about the depression.

4-3. *Loss of Constructive Planning:* I stop planning ahead and thinking about what I am going to do next. I begin to think that the slogan, "One day at a Time," means that I should not plan ahead or think about what I am going to do. I pay less and less attention to details. I become listless. My plans are based more on wishful thinking (how I wish things would be) than reality (how things actually are). As a result I make plans that are not realistic and stop paying attention to the details of implementing those plans.

4-4. *Plans Begin to Fail:* My plans begin to fail and each failure causes new problems. I tend to overreact to or mismanage each problem in a way that creates a new and bigger problem. I start having the same kind of problems with work, friends, family, and money that I used to have when I was using addictively. I feel guilty and remorseful when I have these problems. I work hard to try and solve them, but something always seems to go wrong that creates an even bigger or more depressing problem.

**Phase 5: Immobilization:** During this phase I feel trapped in an endless stream of unmanageable problems and feel like giving up. I can't seem to get started or make myself do the things that I know I need to do.

5-1. *Daydreaming and Wishful Thinking:* It becomes more difficult to concentrate or figure things out. I have fantasies of escaping or "being rescued from it all" by an event unlikely to happen. The "if only" syndrome becomes more

115

common in conversation. I start daydreaming and wishing for things that I want without doing anything to try to get them.

5-2. *Feelings that Nothing Can Be Solved:* I begin to feel like a failure who will never be able to get anything right. The failures may be real or imagined. I exaggerate small problems and blow them out of proportion while failing to notice anything that I do right. I start to believe that "I've tried my best and recovery isn't working out."

5-3. *Immature Wish to Be Happy:* I have a vague desire "to be happy" or to have "things work out" but I don't set up any plans to make those things happen. I want to be happy but I have no idea what I can do to make myself happy. I am not willing to work hard or pay the price for the happiness that I want. I start wishing that something magical would happen to rescue me from my problems.

**Phase 6: Confusion and Overreaction:** During this phase I have trouble thinking clearly and managing my thoughts, feelings, and actions. I am irritable and tend to overreact to small things. The most common relapse warning signs are:

6-1. *Difficulty in Thinking Clearly:* I start to have trouble thinking clearly and solving usually simple problems. Sometimes my mind races and I can't shut it off while at other times it seems to shut off or go blank. My mind tends to wander and I have difficulty thinking about something for more than a few minutes. I get confused and have trouble figuring out how one thing relates to or affects other things. I also have difficulty deciding what to do next in order to manage my life and recovery. As a result I tend to make bad decisions that I would not have made if I were thinking clearly.

6-2. *Difficulty in Managing Feelings and Emotions:* I start to have difficulty managing my feelings and emotions. Sometimes I overreact emotionally and feel too much. At other times I become emotionally numb and can't figure out what I am feeling. Sometimes I feel strange or have "crazy feelings" for no apparent reason. I start to think that I might be going crazy. I have strong mood swings and periodically feel depressed, anxious, and scared. As a result of this, I don't trust my feelings and emotions and often try to ignore stuff or forget about them. My mood sweeps start causing me new problems.

6-3. *Difficulty in Remembering Things:* At times I have problems remembering things and learning new information and skills. Things I want to remember seem to dissolve or evaporate from my mind within minutes. I also have problems remembering key events from my childhood, adolescence, or adulthood. At times, I remember things clearly, but at other times, these same memories will not come to mind. I feel blocked, stuck, or cut off from these memories. At times, the inability to remember things causes me to make bad decisions that I would not have made if my memory were working properly.

6-4. *Periods of Confusion:* I start getting confused more often, and the confusion is more severe and lasts longer. I'm not sure what is right or wrong. I don't know what to do to solve my problems because everything I try seems to make them worse. I get angry at myself because I can't solve my problems and just keep making things worse.

6-5. *Difficulty in Managing Stress:* I start having trouble dealing with stress. Sometimes I feel numb and can't recognize the minor signs of daily stress. At other times I seem overwhelmed by severe stress for no real reason. When I feel stressed out I cannot relax no matter what I do. The things other people do to relax either don't work for me or they make the stress worse. I get so tense that I am not in control. The stress starts to get so bad that I can't do the things I normally do. I get afraid that I will collapse physically or emotionally.

6-6. *Irritation with Friends:* My relationships with friends, family, counselors, and other recovering people become strained. Sometimes I feel threatened when others talk about the changes they are noticing in my behavior and moods. At other times I just don't care about what they say. The arguments and conflicts get worse despite my efforts to resolve them. I start to feel guilty.

6-7. *Easily Angered:* I feel irritable and frustrated. I start losing my temper for no real reason and feeling guilty afterwards. I often overreact to small things that really shouldn't make any difference. I start avoiding people because I am afraid that I might lose control and get violent. The effort to control myself adds to the stress and tension.

**Phase 7: Depression:** During this phase I become so depressed that I can't do the things I normally do. At times I feel that life is not worth living, and sometimes I think about killing myself or using alcohol or other drugs as a way to end the depression. I am so depressed that I can't hide it from others. The most common relapse warning signs are:

7-1. *Irregular Eating Habits:* I either start to overeat or I lose my appetite and eat very little. As a result I start gaining or losing weight. I skip meals and stop eating at regular times. I replace a well-balanced, nourishing diet with "junk food."

7-2. *Lack of Desire to Take Action:* I can't get started or get anything done. At those times, I am unable to concentrate and feel anxious, fearful, uneasy, and often feel trapped with no way out.

7-3. *Difficulty Sleeping Restfully:* I have difficulty sleeping restfully. I cannot fall asleep. When I do sleep, I have unusual or disturbing dreams, awaken many times, and have difficulty falling back to sleep. I sleep fitfully and rarely experience a deep, relaxing sleep. I awaken from a night of sleep feeling tired. The times of day during which I sleep change. At times I stay up late due to an inability to fall asleep and then oversleep because I am too tired to get up in the morning. At times, I become so exhausted that I sleep for extremely long periods, sometimes sleeping around the clock for one or more days.

7-4. *Loss of Daily Structure:* My daily routine becomes haphazard. I stop getting up and going to bed at regular times. I start skipping meals and eating at unusual times. I find it hard to keep appointments and plan social events. I feel rushed and overburdened at times and then have nothing to do at other times. I am unable to follow through on plans and decisions and experience tension, frustration, fear, or anxiety which keeps me from doing what I know needs to be done.

7-5. *Periods of Deep Depression:* I feel depressed more often. The depression becomes worse, lasts longer, and interferes with living. The depression is so bad that it is noticed by others and cannot be easily denied. The depression is most severe during unplanned or unstructured periods of time. Fatigue, hunger, and loneliness make the depression worse. When I feel depressed I separate from other people, become irritable and angry with others, and often complain that nobody cares or understands what I am going through.

**Phase 8: Behavioral Loss of Control:** During this phase I can't control my thoughts, feelings, and behavior. I can't stick to a productive daily schedule. I am still denying how dysfunctional I have become, and I am not willing to admit that I am out of control even though my life is chaotic and I have serious problems. The most common warning signs are:

8-1. *Irregular Attendance at AA and Treatment Meetings:* I start finding excuses to miss therapy and self-help group meetings. I find excuses to justify this and don't recognize the importance of AA and treatment. I develop the attitude, "AA and counseling aren't making me feel better, so why should I make them a number-one priority? Other things are more important."

8-2. *An "I Don't Care" Attitude:* I try to act as if I don't care about the problems that are occurring. This is to hide feelings of helplessness and a growing lack of self-respect and self-confidence.

8-3. *Open Rejection of Help:* I cut myself off from people who can help. I may do this by having fits of anger that drive others away, by criticizing and putting others down, or by quietly withdrawing from others.

8-4. *Dissatisfaction with Life:* Things seem so bad that I begin to think that I might as well go back to alcohol and drug use because things couldn't get worse. Life seems to have become unmanageable even though I am sober and not using addictively.

8-5. *Feelings of Powerlessness and Helplessness:* I have trouble "getting started." I have difficulty thinking clearly, concentrating, and thinking abstractly. I feel that I can't do anything and begin to believe that there is no way out.

**Phase 9: Recognition of Loss of Control:** During this phase my denial breaks and I suddenly recognize how severe my problems are, how unmanageable life has become, and how little power and control I have to solve any of the problems. This awareness is very painful and frightening. By this time, I have become so isolated that it seems that there is no one to turn to for help. The most common warning signs are:

9-1. *Difficulty with Physical Coordination and Accidents:* I start having difficulty with physical coordination that results in dizziness, poor balance, difficulty with hand-eye coordination, or slow reflexes. These problems cause me to feel clumsy and become accident prone.

9-2. *Self-Pity:* I begin to feel sorry for myself and may use self-pity to get attention at AA or from family members. I feel ashamed because I think I must be crazy, emotionally disturbed, defective as a person, or incapable of being or feeling normal. I also feel guilty because I believe I am doing things wrong or failing to work a proper recovery program. The shame and guilt cause me to hide the warning signs and stop talking honestly with others about what I am experiencing. The longer I keep the warning signs hidden, the stronger they become. I try to manage the warning signs and find that I can't do it. As a result, I begin to believe that I must be hopeless and I feel sorry for myself.

9-3. *Thoughts of Social Use:* I start to think that alcohol or drug use will help me feel better. I start hoping that I can one day return to social drinking and recreational drug use. I think I might really be able to control it next time. Sometimes I am able to put these thoughts out of my mind, but often the thoughts are so strong that they cannot be stopped. I may begin to feel that alcohol and drug use is the only alternative to going crazy or committing suicide. Using alcohol and drugs actually looks like a sane and rational alternative.

9-4. *Conscious Lying:* I know that I am lying, using denial, and making excuses for my behavior, but I can't stop myself. I feel out of control. I start doing things on a regular basis that I normally would not do that violate my values. I just can't seem to stop myself or control my behavior.

9-5. *Complete Loss of Self-Confidence:* I feel trapped and overwhelmed because I can't think clearly or do the things I know I need to do to solve my problems. I feel powerless and hopeless. I start to believe that I am useless, incompetent, and will never be able to manage my life.

**Phase 10: Option Reduction:** During this phase I feel trapped by the pain and inability to manage my life. I start to believe that there are only three ways out: insanity, suicide, or self-medication with alcohol or drugs. I no longer believe that anyone or anything can help me. The most common warning signs that occur during this phase are:

10-1. *Unreasonable Resentment:* I feel angry because of the inability to behave the way I want to. Sometimes the anger is with the world in general, sometimes with someone or something in particular, and sometimes with myself.

10-2. *Discontinues All Treatment and AA:* I stop attending all AA meetings. If I am taking Antabuse, I may forget to take it or deliberately avoid taking it regularly. If a sponsor or helping person is part of treatment, tension and conflict develop and become so severe that the relationship usually ends. I may drop out of professional counseling even though I need help and know it.

10-3. *Overwhelming Loneliness, Frustration, Anger, and Tension:* I feel completely overwhelmed. I believe that there is no way out except drinking, suicide, or insanity. I feel like I am helpless, desperate, and about to go crazy.

10-4. *Loss of Behavioral Control:* I experience more and more difficulty in controlling thoughts, emotions, judgments, and behaviors. This progressive and disabling loss of control begins to cause serious problems in all areas of life. It begins to affect my health. No matter how hard I try to regain control, I am unable to do so.

**Phase 11: Alcohol and Drug Use:** During this phase I return to alcohol and drug use, try to control it, lose control, and realize that my addiction is once again destroying my life.

11-1. *Attempting Controlled Use:* I convince myself that I have no choice but to use alcohol and drugs and that using will somehow make my problems better or allow me to escape from them for a little while. I plan to try either social use or a short-term binge. If I try to be a controlled social or recreational user, I start using a little bit on a regular basis. If I decide to go out on a short-term binge, I plan a chemical-use episode that will be a "one-time only, time-limited, controlled binge."

11-2. *Disappointment, Shame, Guilt:* I feel disappointed because alcohol and drugs don't do for me what I thought they would. I feel guilty because I believe that I have done something wrong by using addictively. I feel ashamed because I start to believe that I am defective and worthless as a person and my relapse proves it.

11-3. *Loss of Control:* My alcohol and drug use spirals out of control. Sometimes I lose control slowly. At other times, the loss of control is very rapid. I begin using as often and as much as before.

11-4. *Life and Health Problems:* I start having severe problems with my life and health. Marriage, jobs, and friendships are seriously damaged. Eventually, my physical health suffers and I become so ill that I need professional treatment.

## Relapse Warning Signs for Criminal Behavior

The following list of relapse warning signs has been developed to help chemically dependent criminal offenders to recognize the typical sequence of problems that lead them from a comfortable and stable recovery back to chemical use and criminal behaviors. This list is written in the first person to help you identify with the experiences of relapse prone offenders.

**Phase 1: Internal Change**: During this phase my thinking and feelings begin to change and I know it, but I hide it from others and they don't notice it. The most common warning signs are:

1-1. *Thinking Different:* A part of me starts to think that the straight and sober life is boring and isn't worth the effort. I start thinking about getting back into the old lifestyle, and I know that this thinking will eventually get me into trouble.

1-2. *Feeling Different:* I start to feel bad about being straight and sober. I get bored and feel bad about having to give up the old lifestyle. I keep these feelings to myself and don't tell anyone about them.

1-3. *Acting Different:* I go through the motions of my recovery program, but I am privately disillusioned and start to feel like a phony. I play the game and look like I am doing

123

what I am supposed to do, but underneath I know that it is all a con.

1-4. *Getting Stressed:* I start to feel stressed out and want to get some relief, but nothing I do seems to work. I start craving some excitement or rush that could make the feeling go away, but I don't tell anyone what I am feeling.

**Phase 2: Return of Denial:** During this phase I start to lie and tell myself that everything is going fine and, at times, I start to believe myself. The most common warning signs are:

2-1. *Worrying about Myself:* I get worried about the old way of thinking and feeling that is coming back. I get afraid that I won't be able to handle the straight and sober life. The thought of having to be responsible and accountable gets me down.

2-2. *Denying that I'm Worried:* I tell myself it will all work out. I pretend everything is all right even though I know that it's not. If people ask me about my problems, I tell them that everything is OK. I lie to myself so well that at times I believe it.

**Phase 3: Avoidance and Defensiveness:** During this phase I begin to avoid anyone or anything that will force me to face how messed up my thinking and behavior is getting. If I am confronted I get defensive. The most common warning signs are:

3-1. *Believing I'll Never Get in Trouble Again:* I convince myself that I learned my lesson and I will never do anything illegal again. I tell my friends, family, counselor, and probation officer, "I've really learned this time," even though I don't have a plan for how to change.

3-2. *Needing to Have It My Way:* I think things should go my way because I want them to. I think because other people want me to do well and because I want to do well, things should happen the way I want them to.

3-3. *Privately Putting Others Down:* I make myself feel

better by putting others down. Sometimes I tell people that they don't know anything or are dumb. Most of the time I just think it but don't say it. I tell myself how stupid other people are.

3-4. *Feeling Uncomfortable around "Straight" People:* I feel uncomfortable around people who are not involved in illegal activities. They seem boring and dull. I get nervous and jumpy.

3-5. *Being Alone:* I start avoiding people and spending more time alone. I feel other people are more trouble than they are worth. I wander around alone or go places by myself. Even when I am with other people I feel alone and don't tell anyone what is going on with me. I feel lonely and isolated and start to think that nobody cares.

**Phase 4: Crisis Building:** During this phase I am so isolated and alone that it is easy for me to start setting myself up to get into trouble. The most common warning signs are:

4-1. *Bored and Craving Excitement:* I feel bored with the straight and sober life. I want more excitement, and I start remembering how exciting the old days were and wishing I could have them back.

4-2. *Compulsive Behavior:* I start doing things compulsively to get my mind off my loneliness and my problems. I keep myself too busy to think or notice what I am feeling.

4-3. *Building Up for a Fall:* I feel like I must be the best or I will be nothing. I decide that I will be very successful at everything I do. I get excited and build up in my mind how successful I must be. I feel like if I don't do everything right, I will fail.

4-4. *Not Planning Ahead:* I don't plan the future. When people ask me what my plans are, I tell them what I think they want to hear. I don't know what will happen and I don't really care.

4-5.*Making Bad Decisions:* I make decisions on the spur

of the moment without thinking about what might happen. I think afterwards, "I really screwed up."

4-6. *Nothing Is Going My Way:* When things don't go my way I overreact and blow things out of proportion. I feel like nothing is going my way and nothing will ever be right.

**Phase 5: Immobilization:** During this phase I get so burned out that I stop trying. The most common warning signs are:

5-1. *Bummed Out:* I feel depressed, lonely, and angry. I don't think other people understand. I start having problems sleeping or don't eat regularly and eat junk food. I start to feel afraid and hopeless but believe I can't tell anyone about it.

5-2. *Stop Making an Effort:* I will not do things that I don't like or that are boring or hard for me. I find excuses for not doing things. I don't look into jobs or other things that might help me. I don't feel like maintaining my recovery program.

5-3. *Feeling Like a Zero:* I feel like I am nothing, that I will never be anything, and that everyone knows it.

**Phase 6: Confusion and Overreaction:** During this phase I begin to get confused. I do not know why things are going wrong and lose my temper for no reason. The most common warning signs are:

6-1. *Feeling Put Down:* When other people don't agree with me, don't trust me, or tell me things that I don't want to hear, I see it as a personal put-down and I get angry. I think people should trust me no matter what I may have done in the past or how irresponsibly I am currently acting. I tell them I have changed and expect them to believe me without having to prove myself. I keep my anger to myself.

6-2. *Feeling Like a Victim:* I think that other people are taking advantage of me and there is nothing that I can do about it. I feel picked on and abused. I think that other people will never be satisfied.

6-3. *Blaming Others:* I start to believe that my problems

are caused by others and it is their fault that I am feeling bad. I start resenting other people because things are going so well for them and so poorly for me.

6-4. *Getting Back:* I begin to get back at others by arguing with them, criticizing them, and putting them down. I spend time plotting ways to get even and get away with it.

**Phase 7: Depression:** During this phase I get depressed and bummed out. I stop feeling like doing anything to help myself. The most common warning signs are:

7-1. *Irregular Eating Habits:* I stop eating a healthy diet and start eating junk food and skipping meals. At times I compulsively overeat. At other times I'll miss meals and starve myself.

7-2. *Not Being Able to Sleep Right:* I have trouble sleeping. Sometimes I can't fall asleep. When I do sleep I have strange dreams, wake up many times in the middle of the night, and don't feel rested. Sometimes I get so tired that I sleep the day away.

7-3. *Loss of Daily Structure:* I stop following any regular daily plan. My life becomes confusing and chaotic and I don't care.

7-4. *Periods of Deep Depression:* I have times when I feel very depressed and don't know what to do. Sometimes I think life isn't worth living or I think about killing myself.

**Phase 8: Loss of Control:** During this phase my feelings seem to control me. I can't make myself get back on track. I feel like I can never change, so why should I try? The most common warning signs are:

8-1. *Feeling Afraid but Denying It:* I don't want others to know I am afraid because I think being afraid is being weak. I tell people what I think they want to hear so they won't know how I really feel. Sometimes I tell them I am fine when I am really not.

8-2. *Avoiding Responsibility:* When things go wrong, I tell people, "I forgot," or I do what I want instead of what I told people I would do. I either don't answer them, change the subject, or don't give them an answer. Sometimes I say "yes" when I don't really mean it.

8-3. *Envying Others:* I start thinking about people I know who can still drink, use drugs, break the law, and get away with it. I start to wish that I could do that. I wonder if there is an easier way to do things.

8-4. *Hurting Others:* I hurt other people by what I say and do. When they tell me about it I either get angry and feel picked on or else I can't understand why they should feel hurt by what I did. Sometimes I brush it off and I don't care. Other times I get angry and feel like getting back at them.

8-5. *Pushing Others Away:* When people ask me what is wrong, I tell them that there is nothing wrong. If they persist, I either tell them to leave me alone, yell at them, or do something to make them leave me alone.

**Phase 9: Recognition of Loss of Control:** During this phase I begin to see that I am losing it and that I am not able to stay in control of myself. The most common warning signs are:

9-1. *Wanting to Use Alcohol and Drugs:* I want to use alcohol and drugs to make good feelings better or to get rid of bad feelings. Sometimes I feel good but want to feel better. Sometimes I feel bad and want to escape from my feelings. I keep my thoughts about drinking a secret. Fear of going back to jail if I am caught is the only thing that stops me. If my probation officer, family, or counselor ask me, I lie.

9-2. *Hanging Out with Old Friends:* I start to hang around people who commit crimes. I want to be comfortable and they are the only people I believe understand me. I go back to my old hangouts. I call people I was in jail or prison with. I assure myself that I am only doing this to find out how they are doing.

9-3. *Being Irresponsible:* I miss appointments with my

probation officer, counselor, job interview, or school. I stop attending scheduled activities on my recovery program. I make up excuses as to why I wasn't there. I begin to believe these people are out to get me and I can't trust them.

**Phase 10: Option Reduction:** During this phase I begin to believe that the only choices I have are to kill myself or someone else, to go crazy, or to start using alcohol, drugs, and criminal behavior to feel better and get my way. The most common warning signs are:

10-1. *I Want What I Want, When I Want It:* I think other people should give me what I want and if they don't, I have a right to take it. I feel angry that they won't do what I want or give me what I want. I feel like I have to teach them a lesson. I start thinking about illegal things I can do to get what I want.

10-2. *Believing I Must Win at All Costs:* I feel "high" when I come out on top, even if the fight wasn't important. I will do whatever it takes to get back at someone who I am angry with. I am willing to and do commit crimes just to make me feel on top of things.

10-3. *Refusing to Back Down:* I won't back down when other people don't agree with me even if I know they are right. I am never wrong, no matter what. I feel if I admit to others that I am wrong, they will think I am weak and take advantage of me. Even if I prove to be wrong, I will either leave or start a fight rather than admit it.

10-4. *Losing My Temper:* I start losing my temper if I don't get what I want or if others don't do what I say. I believe I have the right to get angry, threaten, hurt, or get even with other people because they don't understand me or do what I want.

**Phase 11: Criminal Behavior, Alcohol, and Drug Use**: During this phase I start drinking, using illegal drugs, and breaking the law on a regular basis. Sometimes the alcohol and drug use comes first and I use it as an excuse to break the law. At other times I plan to break the law and start using alcohol and drugs to get the courage to do it. The most common warning signs are:

11-1. *Just This Time:* I decide to commit a crime "just this once." It starts with what I consider small things like getting even with someone, committing petty crimes, stealing small things, speeding, or getting into fights. The small stuff doesn't give me the kicks or the excitement that I want, so I plan bigger crimes, but I pick "safe things" and plan carefully so I won't get caught.

11-2. *Using Alcohol and Drugs:* I start using alcohol and drugs. Sometimes I do it to get rid of the depression. At other times I do it to make good times feel better. Alcohol and drugs make it easier for me to get the courage to commit crimes.

11-2. *Things Get Worse:* Soon I start drinking, using drugs, and breaking the law on a regular basis. I am always thinking about how I can get away with something. Things start to get out of hand and I get scared that I will get caught. I can't stop and keep drinking, drugging, and law-breaking. The excitement seems worth the risk.

11-3. *Getting Caught:* I get caught. I get arrested, picked up on a probation or parole violation, or get hurt while drinking or committing a crime. I feel caught by the system. At first I feel like a victim and then I realize that I am right back where I started.

## Using the Warning Sign Lists to Prevent Relapse

These warning signs can be used to help recovering offenders identify and manage warning signs by following a simple procedure. First, ask offenders to read the Relapse Warning Signs for Chemical Dependency and select two warning signs that they identify with. Ask them to explain why they selected those warnings and then write both of those warning signs in their own words with a title and a description.

Then ask offenders to read the Relapse Warning Signs for Criminal Behaviors and select two warning signs that they identify with. Ask them to explain why they selected those warnings, and then write both of those warning signs in their own words with a title and a description.

Then ask offenders to select one of these four warning signs that they would like to analyze in detail. Ask them to describe what they usually think, feel, and have an urge to do when they experience that warning sign. Listen carefully for hidden warning signs that they may bring up.

Ask them to describe a past situation in which this warning sign was problem. Have them tell the situation as if it were a story with a beginning, a middle, and an ending. Probe for details and listen for hidden warnings and other problems that may lead to relapse.

Ask them to describe how they believe that this warning sign may cause problems in the future. Once again, it is important to ask them to tell it like a story with a beginning, a middle, and an ending and to probe for details. Listen once again for hidden warning signs.

Then you give them feedback about the warning signs you heard as they answered your questions. Encourage the offenders to start writing these warning signs down and begin to develop a personal warning sign list. For full details of how to work with the relapse warning sign lists and develop a personal list of warning signs, see *The Relapse Prevention Workbook for the Criminal Offender*.

# Chapter 5

# Building a Recovery Program

Successful recovery for chemically dependent criminal offenders requires four things: (1) a structured lifestyle; (2) a long-term therapeutic relationship; (3) consistent peer group support; and (4) a program of holistic health care.

## A Structured Lifestyle

A structured lifestyle is critical to long-term recovery. Chemically dependent offenders typically live lives centered around the use of alcohol, drugs, and criminal behaviors. When these self-defeating activities are removed, the basic core organizing activities are taken out of their lives. They must be replaced with something more positive or the offender will relapse.

The primary tool for providing the recovering offender with basic life structure is called a *structured recovery program*. An effective recovery program consists of a regular schedule of activities designed to promote stable and responsible living. It also provides a foundation from which to intervene should relapse warning signs develop or the offender relapses to the use of alcohol, drugs, or criminal behaviors.

The recovery program provides a consistent schedule of activities. The less structured the offender's life, the more recovery activities that will be needed to structure it. Unemployed offenders with no stable family unit will require a supervised living program in a halfway house. More stable offenders may work in supervised living programs where they work during the day, attend therapy and self-help activities in the evening, and return to the supervised facility to sleep and for morning check-in. Other offenders may work a regular job and attend recovery activities during the evening and on weekends.

A typical recovery program will consist of a combination of five treatment modalities including group therapy, individual therapy, recovery education, family therapy, and self-help group involvement.

---

## Recovery Program Components
1. Group Therapy
2. Individual Therapy
3. Recovery Education
4. Family Therapy
5. Self-help Groups

---

Group therapy is the core component of treatment. Through involvement in a problem-solving group, recovering offenders learn basic communication and problem-solving skills. They learn how to follow a structured group format, identify and solve problems, and work effectively with other offenders. They also learn how to view structure as a means of getting free from self-defeating behaviors and the personality traits that drive them.

Individual therapy is designed to support involvement in the problem-solving group. It is in individual sessions that offenders learn how to build a positive relationship with a sober and responsible person, the individual therapist. It is best for offenders to have an individual therapist who is either the leader or co-leader of their group. In this way, individual therapy can be designed to support the identification and resolution of problems within the group.

Group and individual therapy are such vital components of the recovery plan that detailed procedures for using them are described later in the chapter.

**Recovery education** consists of structured classes that teach the offender the basics about chemical dependency, criminal personality traits, the recovery process, recovery resources, and how to access them. Recovery education sessions provide straightforward and no-nonsense classes that teach practical information and skills needed for recovery.

The recovery education sessions are structured and include a *pre-test* that measures the basic knowledge that offenders are bringing with them into the session. This is followed by a twenty- to thirty-minute *lecture*. An *educational exercise* is then used to involve the participants in using the information that is presented. This is followed by a discussion of what was learned during the lecture and exercise. The session ends with a *post-test* that measures what was learned during the session.

The participants are held accountable for what they learn. The pre-test and post-test are scored and, if the offender has low scores on the post-test, he or she is expected to take the session over. The level of participation in educational exercises is monitored and the participants' ability to apply the information to their own life circumstances is monitored during the discussion periods.

**Family therapy** is an important component because most offenders eventually leave prison or jail and return to the community. They typically return to a primary or extended family unit of some kind. Offenders typically have ongoing relationships with parents and siblings. They also have spouses or lovers and frequently children, often from a variety of marriages or relationships. As a result, the concept of family therapy needs to be expanded to include these multiple dimensions. Research indicates that appropriate involvement of family members in the offenders' recovery program can lower relapse rates.

**Self-help groups**, such as Alcoholics Anonymous (AA), Narcotics Anonymous (NA), and other Twelve Step programs are a vital component in the offenders' recovery plan. It is through self-help group involvement that offenders begin to expand their recovery program into voluntary and loosely monitored activities. This begins a vital transition from externally imposed and monitored treatment to treatment involvement that is voluntary and self-regulated.

Self-help groups are a vital part of recovery and should be a mandatory part of the recovery program. Twelve Step programs such as AA and NA have been enormously successful in criminal justice settings. Getting offenders actively involved in Twelve Step programs can increase recovery and lower relapse rates. It is recommended that offenders attend a minimum of three Twelve Step meetings each week throughout their supervised recovery period.

Twelve Step programs have been criticized because they are based on a spiritual program of recovery. A number of atheist and agnostic groups have taken legal actions against treatment organizations that fail to offer nonspiritual or secular alternatives to spiritually based support groups such as those based on the Twelve Steps. One such secular support group is Rational Recovery, which is based on the principles of rational emotive therapy.

## A Long-term Therapeutic Relationship

Most chemically dependent offenders have never had a long-term, one-to-one relationship with a sober and responsible adult. Such a relationship provides role modeling, relationship training, and consistent direct positive and negative feedback. This relationship is provided primarily through consistent individual therapy and can be critical for an offender's recovery. A long-term individual relationship can also occur in Twelve Step programs by encouraging recovering persons to find a sponsor who can teach them about the program and be available for private conversations on a regular basis to help them through the rough times of recovery.

**Role modeling** occurs as the offender meets regularly with the same counselor or therapist. They get to see first hand how the counselor deals with them and how they handle problems.

**Relationship training** occurs as the offender learns how to bond with another human being and how to use basic interpersonal skills. By talking about resolving issues and dealing with the feelings that come up in the course of the relationship, the offender can learn how to develop a primary relationship in a healthy way through direct experience. There is no replacement for this immediate experience with a socially responsible adult.

In the context of individual therapy, the offender can receive **consistent direct positive and negative feedback** from a socially responsible adult with whom they have developed a trusting relationship. Offenders become psychologically visible through their feedback and begin to learn how other responsible people perceive their strengths and weaknesses. This new point of view gives them the opportunity to change and gives them a point to compare the feedback from their counselor (a responsible person) with that from their peers.

It is important to remember that the ongoing relationship

with a probation or parole officer can meet some of the needs and accomplish some of the same goals as a one-to-one therapy relationship. The probation or parole officer can develop a healthy, proactive relationship with the offender that provides support, holds them accountable, and allows them to resolve conflicts in a healthy, responsible manner.

## Consistent Peer Group Support

Recovering offenders need to replace peer relationships that are centered on alcohol, drugs, and criminal behaviors with relationships that are centered on recovery. This means getting involved with other people in recovery from chemical dependency and criminal personality traits. The process begins in the therapeutic and group therapy programs and is carried forward in self-help groups, and it eventually leads to developing friendships and sober, responsible networks of friends outside of the treatment context.

Consistent peer feedback is provided in problem-solving group therapy and through involvement in self-help programs. This feedback breaks the pattern of social isolation and allows the offenders to feel connected with other people. It forces the offenders to develop social interest. They have to consistently attend the same group and interact with the same people. They must deal with the long-term impact of their behaviors on others. They can't simply leave when the going gets rough.

The group also provides an experimental laboratory in which they can try out new behaviors. Offenders can act in new and different ways within the groups to see what happens. They can experiment in a safe environment. The peer group also reinforces responsible behavior patterns while providing a source of "credible" confrontation. There is a saying, "You can't con a con." In group therapy, the offenders become visible to themselves through the minds and hearts of other offenders. They tend to respect the feedback they get from their peers because they feel it is honest and being provided by people who know where they are coming from.

## A Program of Holistic Health Care

A holistic health program involves activities that offenders complete to stay healthy, manage stress, and resolve conflicts on a daily basis. These activities are often done alone and include such things as a healthy diet, proper exercise, stress management, recreation and relaxation, and a spiritual program of recovery.

Because group and individual therapy are so important to ongoing recovery, the remainder of this chapter will look in-depth at how to conduct a successful program of group and individual therapy.

## Problem-solving Group Therapy

Problem-solving group therapy is usually the central modality or method of treatment used with chemically dependent criminal offenders. The problem-solving group provides coordination with other treatment modalities, tracks the completion of therapeutic assignments, measures progress, and identifies and resolves problems. It is ideal because it allows a single group leader to work with a larger number of clients. It also provides for peer group support and confrontation that cannot occur in individual therapy.

Clients will often initially resist group therapy because they feel threatened or exposed. It is important to insist on group involvement for most recovering offenders. Group therapy can provide opportunities for communication training, problem solving, and positive peer pressure that are essential for recovery from both chemical dependency and criminal personality traits.

Groups should be viewed as an experimental laboratory in

which the recovering offender can experiment with new, more effective behaviors. Groups should be structured to provide safe and consistent environments. While it is important to point out self-defeating behaviors and their consequences, research has shown that harsh confrontation that tears down defenses and attacks the basic integrity of the offender actually lowers self-esteem and raises the risk of relapse and acting out behaviors after the course of therapy is completed.

It is therefore recommended that group therapy should be structured, directive, and supportive. **Structured groups** follow a standard agenda and allow all group members to know what procedures are going to be followed. It allows them to get comfortable with the group process and master the skills needed to be an effective group member. **Directive groups** expect group members to follow certain procedures. They are told or directed to comply with certain basic rules and responsibilities. They are told how to behave and what to do and are expected to fulfill the behavioral expectations.

---

### Effective Group Therapy Is...
- Structured
- Directive
- Supportive

---

**Supportive groups** seek to find the positive characteristics and behaviors of group members and to reinforce those. The person is separated from the self-defeating behavior. This approach is captured in the statement commonly used in giving feedback: "I can't understand why an intelligent person like you who wants to recover and stay out of jail would use such self-defeating behavior! Can we look at what you did, what motivated you to do it, and what you could do differently in the future?" Notice how this approach supports the person by assuming there is a healthy and motivated person who wants to recover. It does not enable or ignore the self-defeating behavior. It directly says, "You are doing things that are hurting you instead of helping you," and it then invites the offender to look at new and more constructive ways of approaching the problems.

Effective problem-solving groups usually consist of between six and ten offenders. It is important to limit the size of problem-solving groups to assure that all group members have time to work on their problems. The larger the group, the less intense the experience will be for all members. Somewhere between ten and twelve members, a group stops being a group and starts being an audience. At this point genuine interpersonal problem solving is inhibited and only the most extroverted clients are comfortable presenting problems.

Because problem-solving groups are not effective with more than twelve people, other forms of group therapy are suggested if larger groups are needed. Such groups involve lecture and discussion or working with one group member while others observe and ask questions.

Problem-solving groups are usually led by a two-person therapy team consisting of a group leader who is responsible for the group and a co-leader who assists the group leader in leading the group and documenting progress and problems. Group leaders can be trained in a variety of disciplines and can include psychologists, social workers, professional counselors, alcohol and drug abuse counselors, and probation and parole officers. No matter what the professional credentials, it is important that group leaders be trained in problem-solving group therapy methods that support the identification and resolution of problems related to the goal of stopping the use of alcohol, drugs, and criminal behavior and promoting ongoing recovery that results in improvements in biopsychosocial health.

It is important to have two professionals in the group to

avoid manipulation by group members. It must be remembered that many, if not most, chemically dependent offenders have antisocial personality traits. As a result they are charismatic and extremely manipulative. Unless the group leader has another professional in the group, it is easy to lose perspective and get sucked into the denial and manipulation systems of the clients.

Problem-solving groups generally last between one-and-a-half and three hours with a two-hour session being the most common. Sessions shorter than one-and-a-half hours are generally ineffective because there is not enough time to work on issues in depth. By the time the group is warmed up and ready to work, it is over. Sessions longer than three hours tend to be ineffective because group members become tired and stressed and begin to shut down.

To keep group members actively involved in the problem-solving process, there must be clearly stated and enforced group responsibilities, group rules, and a standard group agenda.

### Group Rules and Responsibilities

It is important that each group member understands the basic rules and responsibilities of group members. These rules and responsibilities are not optional or flexible. Chemically dependent people with criminal personality traits tend to test limits and try to manipulate and avoid rules whenever possible. Therefore it is necessary to have strict rules and to enforce them consistently.

The basic rules and responsibilities of group members and the standard agenda should be explained to all group members before they start the group. It is important to get them to verbally agree to comply with these rules and responsibilities. The time to engage in the power struggle is in an individual session before the offender enters the group. Use leverage and threaten consequences up front, in private, before the client enters the group. It saves a lot of group time and avoids unnecessary confrontation and adverse climate setting in the group. If someone doesn't follow the group rules or responsibilities, point it out in group, and then see the group member individually to sort out what is going on and to engage in corrective discipline.

The following is a statement of group responsibilities, group rules, and the standard group format that is often explained to clients before entering the group. It is important to give them a written copy of these statements. Many programs ask the offender to sign a statement indicating that they have reviewed and agree to comply with these responsibilities, rules, and general format. This gives the group leader additional leverage should the recovering offender later refuse to comply. They can show the offender the signed agreement and ask what has changed.

## Group Responsibilities

As a group member you are responsible for:

1. **Giving a reaction at the beginning of each group** by telling the group three things: what you thought about the last group; how you felt about the last group; and the three group members who stood out to you and why. (See the reactions section of the standard group agenda for more information.)

2. **Completing and reporting on assignments:** When you work on a problem or issue in group, the group leader may ask you to complete an assignment to help you make progress in solving that problem. It is your responsibility to complete all assignments in a timely fashion and report what you learned by completing it. (See the report on assignments section of the standard group agenda for more information.)

3. **Presenting problems to the group:** You are expected to present a personal problem or issue to the group at least once every third group session. Recovery implies identifying

and solving personal problems. It is expected that all group members are in group to learn how to solve problems that threaten their sobriety and learn the ability to live a responsible life. (See the problem-solving group process part of the standard agenda for more information.)

4. **Listening when others present problems:** Group members are expected to pay attention and become actively involved when others are presenting problems. This is reflected in active listening during which the other members clarify and paraphrase what they are hearing.

5. **Asking clarifying questions:** Group members are expected to ask at least two or three intelligent and relevant questions to help clarify the problems that other group members present and help identify alternative solutions.

6. **Giving feedback:** Group members are expected to give feedback to other members who are working on problems. This feedback consists of telling the group member what you think his or her problem is and how you feel about him or her as a person.

7. **Completing the closure exercise:** Group members are required to complete a closing exercise at the end of each session by reporting the most important thing that was learned during this session and what they intend to do differently as a result of what they learned.

## Group Rules

The basic rules for problem-solving group therapy are:

1. **Compliance with basic responsibilities:** Membership in the group implies a willingness to comply with the seven basic group responsibilities described above.

2. **Freedom of participation:** Within the constraints of the standard format and basic responsibilities, you can say anything you want any time you want to say it. Other group members have the right to give you feedback about what you

say and how you say it. Silence is not a virtue in this group and can be antitherapeutic.

3. **Right of refusal:** With the exception of refusing to comply with basic group responsibilities, you can refuse to answer any questions or complete any assignments. The group members cannot force you to participate, but they do have the right to express how they feel about your silence or your choice not to get involved.

4. **Confidentiality:** What happens in the group stays among the members, with the exception of the group leaders. Group leaders may consult with other members of the treatment team in order to provide more effective treatment and may report any inappropriate behavior or violation of rules and responsibilities to the appropriate authority. Group members agree not to discuss the content of the problems presented by the other group members with anyone else.

5. **No violence:** Acting out with physical or verbal violence within the group may be grounds for dismissal. Physical violence includes pushing, shoving, or hitting other group members. Verbal violence involves making threats, yelling, using profane language, and name calling. The threat of violence is as good as the act.

6. **No dating or romantic or sexual involvement:** Dating, romantic involvement, or sexual involvement among the members of the group is not allowed. Such activities can sabotage one or both persons' treatment. If such involvement starts to develop, it is to be brought to the attention of the group or the individual counselor at once.

7. **Communication before termination:** Anyone who decides to leave group has a responsibility to inform the group in person before termination.

## Standard Group Agenda
The standard eight-item agenda for problem-solving group

therapy consists of: (1) preparation session, (2) the opening procedure, (3) reactions to last session, (4) report on assignments, (5) setting the agenda, (6) problem-solving group process, (7) the closure exercise, and (8) the debriefing session.

---

### Problem-solving Group Therapy—Standard Agenda

| | |
|---|---|
| 1. Preparation Session | 5. Setting the Agenda |
| 2. The Opening Procedure | 6. Problem-solving Group Process |
| 3. Reactions to Last Session | 7. The Closure Exercise |
| 4. Report on Assignments | 8. The Debriefing Session |

---

1. **Preparation Session:** The group leader prepares for group by reviewing a "thumbnail sketch" of each group member, which includes a review of his or her demographic information and brief history, a review of the problem list and treatment plan, and a review of the issues the patient is most likely to work on in group.

2. **The Opening Procedure:** The group leader establishes a therapeutic group climate by completing an opening procedure. The therapy team enters the group room and seats themselves at opposite sides of the group. They assure that the chairs are arranged so that each group member can easily see everyone else in the group.

New group members are introduced by asking them to report their name and describe in twenty-five words or less why they decided to join the group.

The group leader then conducts a centering exercise by asking everyone to take a deep breath, check what feelings and emotions they are bringing with them into the group, and do a brief body check. This is designed to get the group leader and group members in touch with themselves and leave nonrelated problems outside the group room so they can focus on their current thoughts and feelings. The group leader then asks everyone in the group to open their eyes and to make eye contact with every other group member. The group leader then takes attendance. During the attendance procedure, the group leader establishes intuitive contact by making eye contact and engaging in a brief conversation with each group member.

3. **Reactions from Last Session:** The group leader asks group members to give a reaction to the last session. Each group member is expected to give a reaction from the last session by answering three questions: "What did I think about the last group session?" "How did I feel about the last group session?" "Who are the three group members (other than the group leaders) who stood out to me from last session and why did they stand out?"

---

### Reactions to Last Session
- What I thought about last session is ....
- How I felt about last session is ....
- The three people who stood out and why they stood out are ....

---

The reactions are not merely a report of what took place in the last session, but a description of the feelings and thoughts generated in the members as a result of being in group. The reactions should indicate if the members were able to transfer what they learned during the last session into their daily lives.

A typical reaction made by a group member to the last meeting would be as follows: "I thought last week's group was very productive. I learned a lot about how I deal with anger and frustration. There was a lot of good feedback when I talked about my problem. I had a feeling of accomplishment as I worked on my problems. I was surprised. I got excited instead of depressed for the first time in a long time."

147

"Joe, you stood out to me because you understood what I was talking about. Mary, you stood out because you told me that you cared about me. I'm not sure if I believe you. A part of me thought you were telling the truth and I felt good. Another part of me said, 'Why should she care—no one else does.' I'm still not sure if you were being honest or just saying what you thought I wanted to hear. Pete, I was upset with you because you didn't seem to pay attention to me when I was talking."

It takes time for the average group member to learn how to give good reactions in group. This learning takes place as a result of instruction and imitation. The group leader and other group members should explain the components of a good reaction to each new group member. A written handout should be provided that describes the components of a reaction and gives examples. The group member will also learn by observing and imitating the reactions of other group members.

The following guidelines can help group members give good reaction: (1) When reporting your thoughts, start the sentence with the words, "I think...". (2) When reporting your feelings, start the sentence with the words, "I feel ..." or "I am experiencing ...". (3) Take time to breathe before and during your reactions so you can stay centered and in touch with your feelings. Pause briefly and take a deep breath. Notice the feelings in your throat, chest, and stomach. Breathe again and notice your thoughts (the self-talk or silent conversation going on in your head). Breathe again and notice any memories. Feel free to share any of these as they occur. (4) When giving feedback to others, look at them and make direct eye contact, and talk in the first person (in other words, use the word "you" instead of the words "he," "she," or "they").

4. **Report on Assignments:** Assignments are an important part of the problem-solving group therapy. The goal of group is to identify problems that group members wish to resolve

and then to set up an action plan for their resolution. Continuity in the problem-solving process is created by the use of assignments that allow the member to work on the problem between group sessions and then report on their progress.

A member completes a report on an assignment by answering the following questions:

*"What assignment did you have and what did you hope to learn by completing it?"* This question assures that the group member remembers what the assignment was and understands the goal in completing the assignment.

*"Did you complete the assignment?"* This question holds group members directly responsible for completing the assignment. If group members completed the assignment, they are asked, *"What did you learn from completing the assignment?"* This is a brief report that shouldn't take longer than a minute to complete. I often ask the member to answer this question "in twenty-five words or less." If it is obvious the member needs to process a lot of information, the exploration of the assignment should be entered on the agenda for later work during the problem-solving portion of that group.

If group members fail to complete the assignment they are asked, *"Why didn't you complete the assignment?"* If resistance appears to be part of the failure to complete the assignment and the group leader feels a need to process the resistance in depth, the discussion should be entered on the agenda for later work during the problem-solving portion of that group.

As a rule, group leaders only get what they "expect and inspect." It is the group leader's responsibility to expect the group members to meet their responsibilities. The group leader does this by giving assignments (expecting progress toward problem resolution), keeping records of all therapeutic assignments, and assuring that these assignments are monitored (inspected) until the issue is resolved or the assignment

149

is officially changed or discontinued by the group leader in group.

Group members are responsible for completing all assignments they agree to complete. Problem solving in group is a collaborative process and group members have the right to negotiate what assignments they take on. Once they agree to complete an assignment, however, they are held responsible for meeting that commitment unless the group leader, the group members, and clients agree that it is not useful to further pursue the issue.

5. **Setting the Agenda:** After all assignments have been reviewed, the group leader sets the agenda by asking, "Who has an issue to work on in group?" An issue can be either a new problem the group member wants to bring up, the completion of an assignment from a previous group, or the completion of standard exercise from some standard workbook such as *The Relapse Prevention Workbook for the Criminal Offender.*

---

### Setting the Agenda
- Who wants to work?
- What do you want to work on?
- Is it an emergency?

---

Group members who have issues to work on indicate so at this time. The group leader will ask for a brief (twenty-five words or less) description of the problem and will ask if this is an emergency issue that must be dealt with immediately. The goal is to learn enough about the problem to be presented so it can be correctly prioritized when the agenda is set. The group leader will identify all the members who want to work and establish the order in which people will work, dealing with emergency issues first. Group members who do not have time to complete their work in this group session will be first on the agenda in the following group session. Care needs to be taken not to begin the problem-solving process until all people with issues to work on have been identified.

6. **Problem-solving Process:** One person works at a time with the entire group involved in the problem-solving process. A standard problem-solving process is used that consists of five steps: These are:

*Problem presentation:* The group members present their problems to the group. The initial presentation of the problem is often vague, general, and incomplete. The member is asked several times, "Is there anything else we need to know to help you solve the problem?" When the member either begins repeating or states he or she doesn't have anything else, the group begins to ask clarifying questions.

*Group questioning:* The group begins to ask clarifying questions using an active listening model. The goal is to clarify generalizations, deletions, and distortions in the original presentation of the problem. A *generalization* is a statement that is all-inclusive, such as "Everything is going wrong!" This is challenged by asking the clarifying question, "What do you mean everything is going wrong? Can you be more specific and give us an example of exactly what is going wrong?"

A *deletion* is a statement that fails to give necessary information. A group member may say, for example, "I got angry." This is an incomplete statement because it fails to explain who he got angry at, what the person did that caused him to become angry, and how he acted out his anger. This is challenged by asking the clarifying questions: "Who did you get angry with? What did they do that caused you to get angry? What did you do after you got angry?"

A *distortion* is a statement that blows something out of proportion or distorts the real facts. Distortions often involve figures of speech that are not helpful in solving a problem. A group member may say, "He blew me away!" This is a distortion because, in reality, the person was not blown away. The clarifying question, "What exactly did the person do that blew you away?" can be used. Another example would be a group member who says, "He treated me like crap." Again the question, "What exactly did he do to treat you like crap?" can help clarify.

The use of *open-ended questions* is strongly encouraged for drawing out information. An open-ended question is one that cannot be answered by a yes-or-no answer. A *closed question* is one that must be answered by a yes-or-no answer. Closed questions give very little information. Open-ended questions give much more information. The question, "Are you married?" is a closed question that will tell very little. This can be turned into an opened-ended question by asking, "Tell me what your current love relationship is like?" This will give far more information.

Closed questions are recommended for getting a commitment to confirm or deny specific information. For example, after the group member describes his or her relationship, you might ask the question, "Are you saying that alcohol and drugs have caused problems in your marriage?" This use of closed questions forces the person being asked to make a commitment to a definite and specific answer.

It is important to keep the focus on the issue of staying abstinent from alcohol, drugs, and criminal behaviors. To do this the group members need to learn how to ask *problem-focused questions*.

When dealing with chemically dependent criminal offenders the following problem-focused questions can be used:

- When was the last time you used alcohol, drugs, or criminal behaviors?

- When was the last time you had an urge or desire to use alcohol, drugs, or criminal behaviors?
- What problems or situations created the urge to start using alcohol, drugs, or criminal behaviors?
- How does the problem you are currently working on relate to your use of alcohol, drugs, or criminal behaviors?
- How does the problem you are currently working on affect your ability to recognize that you have a serious problem with alcohol, drugs, and criminal behaviors and needed to stop drinking, drugging, and committing crimes?
- How did this problem affect your willingness or ability to stay abstinent from alcohol, drugs, and criminal behavior and maintain your recovery program?
- How did this problem set you up to start using alcohol, drugs, or criminal behavior in the future?

***Therapeutic processing by the group leader (if appropriate):*** The group leader may use a specific therapy technique to assist the patient in the problem-solving process. The most commonly used techniques involve guided imagery for mental rehearsal and role playing for skill training. Care should be taken not to make the group dependent upon the leader to resolve all issues. It is recommended that the leader use individual techniques not more often than every two to three patients who work in group. At times, the therapeutic processing may occur after feedback from the group members.

***Group feedback:*** The group members will each give feedback to the member who worked by answering two questions: (1) "What is your understanding of the problem that this person is working on?" (2) "After listening to the person work on the problem, how do you feel about him (or her) as a person?" The group leader will often ask group members to give feedback by completing two statements: (1) "I think that your problem is ...", and (2) "My feelings about you as a person are ...".

153

As group members get better at giving feedback, the leader can also ask them to tell the problem solver the strengths they see that will help solve the problems and the weaknesses they see that may get in the way of solving the problem. This can be done by asking the group member giving the feedback to complete two statements: (1) "The strengths I see that will help you to solve the problem are...", and (2) "The weaknesses I see that will interfere with your solving the problem are...".

Each group member should be allowed no more than two or three minutes to give feedback. Group members need to learn how to get to the point, say what they mean, and then move on. Most group members will tend to get sidetracked and go on forever when giving feedback. The group leader must focus them on the main points of feedback. It is important to remember that there is a limited amount of group time. If each member in an eight-person group spends two minutes giving feedback, that will take sixteen minutes or half of the allotted time for the person to work on a problem. It is also important to remember that the person receiving the feedback has limits to what he or she can integrate and remember. Feedback that is short, clear, and concise is more likely to be remembered.

*Summary and assignment by the group leader:* The group leader will summarize the main points of feedback given by the group. The group leader will often begin this summary by saying, "Let me summarize what I am hearing the group tell you." The leader should limit the major points of feedback to the three most important points the problem solver needs to hear. The group leader will then help the problem solver develop an assignment that will help him or her to progress in the problem-solving process. The process of giving assignments will be described in more detail later in this chapter when we review the problem-solving process.

Not every person will work on a problem during each

session, but this doesn't mean that they are not benefiting from attendance. There is an 80/20 rule for group treatment: 80 percent of the benefit of group treatment occurs from learning how to become responsibly involved in helping others to solve their problems. In other words, most group members get more benefit out of listening to the problems of other group members, asking questions, and giving feedback than they do out of working on their own issues. Only 20 percent of the benefit is derived from working on personal problem issues.

During the problem-solving section of group, all members have the responsibility to listen to other group members' problems, ask relevant questions to clarify the problem, give feedback about what they think the problem is and how they feel about the person after listening to how they presented the problem, and share personal experiences with similar problems when appropriate. Self-disclosure must be carefully managed to keep the primary focus upon the patient who is working on the issue.

## The Standard Problem-solving Process

A problem is rarely solved in one group presentation. To solve a single problem requires three to six group presentations. As a result, each problem needs to be broken down into chunks that can be worked on in twenty- to thirty-minute segments. In order to break the problem down, we need to understand a standard problem-solving process. This standard process should be used in both group and individual therapy, and it consists of three general steps: (1) problem identification and clarification; (2) identification of alternatives and consequences; and (3) decision, action, and evaluation.

## The Standard Problem-solving Process
1. Problem identification and clarification
2. Identification of alternatives and consequences
3. Decision, action, and evaluation

The first step in problem solving is **problem identification and clarification.** When group problem solvers (the members in group who are presenting a problem) identify a problem, they are being asked to answer the question, What is the problem and how it is affecting you? At this stage the problem is usually vague and general because the problem solver knows that something is wrong but can't clearly explain what is wrong. The process of clearly explaining what the problem is leads naturally into problem clarification.

The group begins clarifying the problem by asking, "Is there anything else that we need to know to help you solve the problem?" They then ask questions about the details of the problem and how the problem relates to the problem solver's use of alcohol, drugs, and criminal behaviors. Typical clarifying questions involve what I call the who, what, when, where, why, and how questions. *Who* is involved in this problem? *What* are you or other people doing that is causing or complicating the problem? *When* did this problem first start? *Why* are you interested in solving the problem right now? Why didn't you solve it yesterday or put it off until tomorrow? *How* is this problem affecting you or other people?

A good clarifying strategy is to ask the group member to tell a story about how this problem occurred in the past and how it is likely to occur in the future. By listening carefully to the stories, the leaders and group members can often hear aspects of the problem that would remain hidden otherwise. The current problem can also be related to other things in the offender's life by asking, "What other problems are there in your life that are similar to or related to this problem?"

Remember to keep the focus on alcohol, drugs, and criminal behaviors by asking about how the problem can create an urge to relapse, discourage the problem solver from practicing his or her recovery program, or activate addictive or criminal thinking.

Problem identification and clarification usually takes two group sessions. In the first session the offender presents the problem and responds to questions. The answers typically show that the offender is confused about the problem and really isn't sure about what is going on. This general confusion is presented to the client in the feedback from other group members.

The group leader then gives the offender an assignment to clarify the problem. This often involves writing a problem statement or interviewing other group members who have had similar problems. In the second group they present the problem again, and this time they can usually clarify the problem sufficiently to start looking at alternative solutions.

The second step of problem solving involves **identifying alternatives and consequences**. The problem solver is told that there is always more than one way to solve a problem. Good problem solvers usually can identify at least three different ways of solving the problem that have a good chance of working. These different ways of solving a problem are called *alternatives*.

Alternative solutions are identified by asking group members to find out what the problem solver has done in the past to try to solve this problem and which of those past efforts were helpful and which were not helpful. Group members can also explain what they have done in the past when they have had a similar problem or what they know that other people have tried. The problem solver and other group members are then asked what new ideas they can come up with that could help to solve this problem. The problem solver should write a list of the alternative solutions identified during the group.

Each alternative solution will produce different consequences if the problem solver attempts to use it. Although you cannot precisely predict what will happen, logical thinking will determine a best possible outcome, a worst possible outcome, and a most likely outcome. This can then become an assignment: take each alternative solution and identify the best, the worst, and the most likely things that could happen if you tried to solve the problem this way.

Typically, the process of identifying alternatives and consequences will take two or three group sessions. In the first session the group helps the problem solver to write an initial list of alternative solutions. The group leader gives the problem solver an assignment to interview at least three other people he or she knows who have had similar problems and write down what they have done to solve the problems.

In the second group session the problem solver brings back the list of alternative solutions. The group then begins to ask questions about the logical consequences of using each of the alternatives. Generally, the group can easily identify alternative solutions that are based on addictive or criminal thinking that would make the problem worse. These failed alternatives need to be pointed out and eliminated from the list. The best three alternatives are identified.

The problem solver is given the assignment to project the best, worst, and most likely outcomes of those three alternative solutions. In the third group session these logical outcomes are explored and the problem solver moves into the next step of problem solving.

The third and final step involves **decision, action, and evaluation**. With this information problem solvers must decide which alternative solution they will use. This can be accomplished by instructing the group to ask the following questions: What alternatives do you plan to use to try to solve this problem? How will you put that solution into action (what steps are you going to take)? Who else needs to be involved in attempting to solve this problem? When will you take action (name a specific date and time)?

They must then take action and try to solve the problem by using the identified alternative and evaluate if the alternative worked. Even when problems are carefully thought through, the alternative selected doesn't always work. If the alternative fails, it is eliminated from the list and a new alternative is chosen.

Evaluation usually takes place by asking the problem solver the following questions: What exactly did you do? How closely were you able to follow your original plan? How well did the attempted solution work? Was the problem solved or do you need to try another alternative?

It usually takes a minimum of two or three groups to complete the decision, action, and evaluation steps of problem solving. In the first group the person decides what alternatives to use. He or she then explains in detail how to implement it. Many times the group leader will use mental rehearsal or role-playing techniques to give the problem solver the opportunity to practice solving the problem in group before he or she actually tries it in the real world.

The problem solver may also be given an assignment to practice the solution in a safe environment before doing it for real. Such assignment could involve expressing anger to an AA sponsor before going home and attempting to express anger at a spouse. The person comes to the second group and reports on how the practice assignment went, discusses any concerns, and receives the assignment to try the solution for real. In the third group the problem solver reports on how well the alternative worked.

The following table summarizes the group problem-solving process and how it unfolds over a series of groups.

| Group # | Group Action | Assignment |
|---|---|---|
| **Step 1: Problem Identification and Clarification** | | |
| Group #1 | Present problem and answer clarifying questions | Write a clarified problem statement |
| Group #2 | Present clarified problem to group | Write list of alternative solutions |
| **Step 2: Identify Alternatives and Consequences** | | |
| Group #3 | Present alternative solutions and start identifying consequences | Interview three people who have solved similar problems |
| Group #4 | Review alternatives and select the best three | Project the best, worst, and most likely outcome to the three alternatives |
| **Step 3: Decision, Action, Evaluation** | | |
| Group #5 | Select best alternative and discuss or practice implementation | Practice alternative in safe and low-risk setting |
| Group #6 | Report on problems and progress with practice sessions | Use the alternative in real life situation |
| Group #7 | Report on outcome | |

This may seem like a tedious process, but it is absolutely essential if chemically dependent offenders are to recover. As a general rule, chemically dependent offenders have poor problem-solving skills (they don't know how to solve problems), poor impulse control (they don't think things through before they act), very poor self-discipline (they do what they want, when they want to instead of following orderly processes that work), and difficulty in learning from past experience (they create a mess and never stop to think about what they did that caused it).

As you can see, this process addresses all these issues by forcing chemically dependent offenders to think things through before they act and to control their impulse to act out

160

without thinking first. It also forces recovering offenders to evaluate what happened as a result of their actions and to begin identifying cause-and-effect relationships between what they do and what happens as a result. This means they are forced to start learning from their past experiences.

During a typical problem-solving session in a single group, two or three members will work on solving a problem. Each group member will work for twenty to forty minutes. The group leader typically gives the problem solver about fifteen minutes to present the problem and respond to group questioning. The next fifteen minutes are reserved for feedback from group members and time for the group leader to summarize the feedback and work with the problem solver to create an assignment to move to the next step in problem solving.

7. **The Closure Exercise:** At the end of the group the leader uses a closure exercise that asks members to complete a form by answering two questions: "What is the most important thing I have learned in this group session?" and "What am I going to do differently as a result of what I have learned?"

---

### The Closure Exercise
- The most important thing I learned in group is....
- What I am going to do differently as a result of what I learned is....

---

All group members complete the form, give a copy of it to the group leader, and tell the group how they answered the questions. The group leader documents on the bottom of each form for entry in the record. The time and place of the next group is confirmed and group is adjourned.

8. **The Debriefing Session:** The debriefing session is designed to review the patients' problems and progress, prevent

therapy team burnout, and improve the group skills of the therapy team. A brief review of each patient is completed, outstanding group members and events are identified, progress and problems discussed, and the personal feelings and reactions of the therapy team reviewed.

## Individual Therapy

Experience with problem-solving group therapy shows that groups run more efficiently and effectively when group members have individual sessions designed to support the ongoing group process. This is especially true when the group members are highly resistant, have high levels of denial, or have difficulty learning from past experience or maintaining a consistent direction in solving a problem. Because chemically dependent criminal offenders fit all of these characteristics, it is important to conduct individual sessions that support the ongoing problem-solving group process.

Offenders are more likely to comply with established group procedures if they have met one or more times with the group leader before entering the group. This allows the group leader to establish his or her authority, explain the problem-solving group process, and establish a clear contract for participation. The group contract should be based on clearly identified problem issues related to the use of alcohol, drugs, and criminal behaviors. A step-by-step plan should be created that will be used to solve those problems. Offender must believe that being in group can help them deal with problems that are troubling them. This process of identifying the initial problems and proposing ways the group can assist in solving them helps motivate the offender and lower resistance during the first several groups.

The primary goals of individual therapy are to provide a consistent one-to-one therapeutic relationship with the offender. It is important to remember that the group leader may be one of the few sober, responsible people the offender has ever had a close personal relationship with. If the offender can interact in a positive way with the group leader and accept the group leader as a role model, progress in recovery will progress far more rapidly. Spending time with the offender individually allows this bonding process to occur more quickly and generally makes the group member far more receptive to working productively in a group and far less likely to sabotage the work of other group members.

## Standard Agenda for Individual Therapy

There is a recommended standard agenda for individual sessions that consists of: reactions to last session, a recovery check, assignment review, group preparation, and topic-oriented conversation. Let's look at each item on this agenda.

**Reactions to last session** is a procedure that is very similar to the reactions presented in group. Offenders are asked what they thought about their last individual and group session, how they felt about the last session, and what they have been doing differently as result of the therapy they have been receiving. This procedure focuses the offender on doing something different and on positive change in between sessions as a primary goal of recovery.

---

**Agenda for Individual Therapy**

| | |
|---|---|
| 1. Reactions to Last Session | 4. Group Preparation |
| 2. Recovery Check | 5. Topic-oriented |
| 3. Assignment Review | Conversation |

---

The counselor then leads the offender through a **recovery check,** which involves asking the client to answer the following questions:

• Have you used alcohol or other mood-altering drugs since our last session?

• Have you engaged in any criminal or antisocial behaviors since our last session?

• Have you had the urge or compulsion to use alcohol, drugs, or criminal behaviors since your last group or individual session?

• Have you attended all of the scheduled activities on your recovery plan?

• Have you experienced any resistance or resentments about maintaining your recovery plan?

This recovery check allows the counselors to quickly identify any serious relapse warning signs that may threaten the offender's ongoing recovery. It also keeps the focus clearly on doing what is necessary to avoid relapsing back into the use of alcohol, drugs, and criminal behaviors.

The next part of the session is devoted to an **assignment review**. This is completed by asking the offender what assignment he or she is working on and the problems and progress they are experiencing while working on it. Because the assignment is directly related to the treatment plan, this procedure keeps a clear problem focus. If the offender is not working on an assignment, or doesn't remember what it is, this becomes a critical issue.

The next part of the session is devoted to **group preparation**. The counselor works with the offender to develop a plan for how to present the issue in group. This group preparation also involves instruction and practice at basic group skills such as how to give a reaction, how to do active listening, how to ask an open-ended question, how to give feedback, and how to do the closure exercise. This group preparation should be based on a skill-building philosophy. Group members must learn the skills needed to carry out their responsibilities in group. The individual session can help them build those skills.

For offenders who are actively involved in their recovery, the individual session is entirely devoted to reactions, the recovery check, assignment review, and group preparation. Resistant offenders, however, often have very little to say about these things. As a result, the therapist should always be prepared with **topic-oriented conversation** to use should the offender have nothing else to work on. These topics can cover broad areas such as recognition and acceptance of chemical dependency and criminal personality traits, how it feels to comply with a recovery program, denial and resistance, or specific symptoms of chemical dependency and criminal personality traits. The topics should be selected to match issues that are being experienced by the offender.

Now that we have reviewed the basic group and individual therapy procedures, we can look at how to use the specific relapse prevention exercises from *The Relapse Prevention Workbook for the Criminal Offender.*

## Chapter 6

# Relapse Prevention Therapy with Criminal Offenders

This chapter will describe a detailed model for doing Relapse Prevention Therapy (RPT) based on the CENAPS Model of Recovery and Relapse Prevention. The CENAPS Model is a structured method of recovery and relapse prevention that has been under clinical development since the early 1970s. It is designed to work effectively independent of the personality of the counselor or therapist using it. If the method is used as described, it will work equally well for any counselor or therapist who has adequate helping characteristics and average or above basic counseling skills.

The CENAPS Model of Recovery and Relapse Prevention guides people through a four-part clinical protocol: self-assessment, warning sign identification, warning sign management, and recovery planning. The method works best with clients who recognize and accept that they are suffering from both chemical dependency and criminal or antisocial personality and have expressed a desire to abstain from alcohol, drugs, and criminal behaviors. Many relapse prevention specialists, however, have reported that the CENAPS Model is effective in breaking denial and helping people recognize that they are chemically dependent and cannot safely use alcohol or drugs (Downing, 1991).

This chapter will describe the basic procedure for using the exercises in *The Relapse Prevention Workbook for the Criminal Offender* (part 3 of this series). Although this chapter can be used without the workbook, it is strongly recommended that the techniques described in this chapter be used with offenders by guiding them through the workbook exercises.

This workbook is designed to be used as part of a structured recovery program. The format of the workbook is simple and, upon superficial review, it would seem that recovering offenders could complete it on their own. Most recovering offenders, however, will not complete the workbook unless they are involved in structured classes, group therapy, or individual therapy sessions that hold them accountable for completing the exercises and help them to process the feelings and reactions that get stirred up by the process. This is because the exercises focus the recovering offender on issues that stir deep feelings and can activate denial and resistance. In an unsupervised setting, most recovering offenders will stop working on the exercises as soon as they encounter these difficult issues.

A typical relapse prevention program would involve a number of phases:

**Phase 1: Stabilization:** During this phase recovering offenders are detoxified from the effects of alcohol and drugs and stop using criminal behavior. They also complete an evaluation for both chemical dependency and criminal personality traits. If clients have a high level of recognition of their chemical dependency and criminal personality traits, a desire to stay sober and stop using criminal behaviors, have had previous treatment and efforts at recovery, then they are

167

ready to enter phase 2 of the relapse prevention therapy program. If clients are in denial of their chemical dependency or criminal personality, lack motivation to recover, or are disruptive, they will require treatment in a transitional counseling or primary recovery program before completing relapse prevention therapy. If a recovering offender meets the criteria, he or she can move into phase 2.

**Phase 2: Relapse Prevention Education:** During this phase the recovering offender is entered into a structured education program that: (1) describes the symptoms of chemical dependency and criminal personality; (2) describes the recovery process from both disorders; (3) describes the common warning signs that lead back to the use of alcohol, drugs, and criminal behavior; and (4) describes how to develop both a primary recovery plan and a relapse prevention plan.

This educational phase helps recovering offenders think through their life, addiction, and criminal history in a general way. It gives them new ideas and new ways of thinking about their problems. It also allows them to begin interacting in a classroom setting with other recovering offenders to begin building appropriate social skills in a low threat environment.

A structured education program called the *Staying Sober Recovery Education Modules* is available from Herald House/Independence Press (P.O. Box 1770, 3225 South Noland Road, Independence, MO 64055-0770; 1-800-767-8181 or 816/252-5010). This resource provides structured education sessions complete with lecture outlines, overhead slides, pre-tests, post-tests, and educational exercises. It also explains the basic principles of adult education and how to structure individually designed education programs based on the material that can range from eight to thirty-two sessions.

Although the length and intensity of the education can vary, chemically dependent criminal offenders seem to do better with three educational sessions per week for a period of six to eight weeks.

**Phase 3: Relapse Prevention Plan Development:** During this phase the client completes the exercises in *The Relapse Prevention Workbook for the Criminal Offender* and is involved in problem-solving group therapy and individual therapy. There are four primary goals: (1) to identify the core lifestyle patterns that lead to relapse by completing an in-depth review of their life, addiction, and criminal history; (2) to develop a comprehensive list of personal warning signs that lead from sober, responsible living back to the use of alcohol, drugs, and criminal behavior; (3) to identify critical warning signs and develop warning sign management strategies that will allow them to cope with these warning signs without returning to the use of alcohol, drugs, or criminal behavior; and (4) to develop a structured recovery program that will support the ongoing identification and management of relapse warning signs.

This phase is generally structured in a process involving twenty-four problem-solving group therapy sessions, each three hours in duration, and twelve individual counseling sessions. The sessions are normally scheduled three times per week for eight weeks.

**Phase 4: Warning Sign Identification and Management:** This phase consists of two, two-hour group therapy sessions per week for eight weeks. The goal is for the recovering offenders to complete daily inventory exercises in which they monitor for the presence of warning signs. Recovering offenders report the warning signs that they identify and what they did to manage them. New warning signs are identified and the recovering offenders are supported in developing a long-term recovery plan.

## The Clinical Process

During phase 3 (Relapse Prevention Plan Development), recovering offenders use a structured process for completing and processing the exercises in *The Relapse Prevention Workbook for the Criminal Offender*. This process follows these steps:

1. **Completing a workbook exercise:** The recovering offender is assigned an exercise in *The Relapse Prevention Workbook for the Criminal Offender*. These assignments can be given in group or individual sessions. These exercises are completed as written assignments.

2. **Reviewing the assignment with a senior recovering offender:** The recovering offender is assigned to review the exercise he or she completed with another group member who has already successfully completed the exercise and processed it in a group or individual therapy session. This is therapeutic for both the recovering offender who is working on the exercise and the senior recovering offender who is providing assistance.

This review process is highly structured. First, the senior recovering offender presents the exercise that was completed, explains how it was processed in individual and group therapy, and explains what was learned as a result of completing the exercise. Next, the recovering offender presents the completed exercise to the senior recovering offender and asks for feedback. The session ends by the senior recovering offender helping the new recovering offender to prepare to present his or her exercise for processing in group and individual therapy.

3. **Processing in group and individual sessions:** There is a structured procedure for processing exercises in group and individual therapy. The purpose of processing the exercises is to help the recovering offender learn and integrate new information. It is important to ask the recovering offender to

do more than simply report factual answers to questions on the exercises.

Processing focuses on answering two questions: (1)What did you learn about yourself by completing the assignment? and (2) What are you going to do differently as a result of what you learned?

When an issue is processed in individual therapy, the therapists check to be sure that the recovering offender completed the exercise. They then ask the offender to describe what he or she learned by completing the exercises. The therapist will then identify specific issues that should be part of group processing. The recovering offender is then instructed on how to process the issue in group.

When an issue is processed in group therapy the recovering offender completes a four-step process: (1) They present the exercise to the group and what they learned in competing the exercise; (2) the group asks clarifying questions keeping the focus strictly on discovering information that will help the recovering offender identify warning signs that lead to relapse and manage them more effectively; (3) the group gives the recovering offender feedback by telling him or her what was learned about the recovering offender from this exercise and how they feel about the recovering offender; and (4) the therapist summarizes the feedback and gives the recovering offender an assignment to move on to the next step of relapse prevention therapy.

The rest of this chapter will review how to use the exercises in *The Relapse Prevention Workbook for the Criminal Offender* and is divided into four sections that correspond with the sections of the workbook. These are:

Section I: Self-Assessment
Section II: Warning Sign Identification
Section III: Warning Sign Management
Section IV: Recovery Planning.

## Section I: Self-Assessment

During this part of relapse prevention therapy, clients complete a series of structured self-assessment exercises that helps them examine their presenting problems, current symptoms of chemical dependency and criminal personality, life, addiction, and criminal history, and recovery and relapse history. The primary goals of self-assessment are:

1. to help offenders determine if they are suffering from chemical dependency, criminal personality traits, or both;

2. to review the developmental life history and identify the core lifestyle issues that promoted the development of chemical dependency and criminal personality traits; and

3. to develop an in-depth understanding of how repetitive self-defeating lifestyle patterns are related to their tendency to relapse to the use of alcohol, drugs, and criminal behaviors.

These goals are achieved by guiding the recovering offender through the completion of the following exercises.

### *Exercise #1: Alcohol and Drug Addiction Test*

The Alcohol and Drug Addiction Test was adapted from the symptoms of chemical dependency described in the Jellinek Chart. The symptoms were rewritten in language that would be easy for the offender to identify with. The more symptoms checked when offenders take the test, the more likely they are to be chemically dependent.

It is recommended that the Alcohol and Drug Addiction Test be used with other objective tests for chemical dependency such as the CAGE Questionnaire (Mayfield et al., 1974; Ewing, 1984), the Michigan Alcoholism Survey Test (MAST) (Selzer, 1971), or the Self-administered Alcoholism Screening Test (SAAST) (Swensen and Morris, 1975). For a summary on how to use these and other instruments to complete a comprehensive alcoholism diagnostic procedure, see chapter 8 in the *Seventh Special Report to the U.S. Congress on Alcohol and Health* (U.S. Department of Health and Human Services, 1990, pp. 181-199).

The Alcohol and Drug Addiction Test helps recovering offenders identify if they have a problem with alcohol or drugs. Recovering offenders must recognize their chemical dependency and make a commitment to abstain from alcohol and drugs before relapse prevention therapy can be effective.

Recovering offenders complete this test and process the results in individual counseling and group therapy. They are asked if they agree with the results, what thoughts and feelings were stirred up by taking this test, and listening to what the results mean.

It is important to discuss how offenders think their alcohol and drug use is related to their criminal behaviors. The primary goal is to get recovering offenders to examine their symptoms of addiction and to begin making a connection between their use of alcohol and drugs and their current legal problems.

If offenders show definite symptoms of chemical dependency but deny that they are chemically dependent, they should be asked to explain why they believe that they are not chemically dependent. It is helpful to clarify their personal definition of chemical dependency by having them write it down and then compare it to the information on the test.

Many addicts have a standard definition of an alcoholic or drug addict that allows them to keep drinking and drugging. In their minds, an alcoholic or addict is someone who uses significantly more alcohol and drugs than they do! This definition needs to be challenged.

It is important to help recovering offenders connect their alcohol and drug use with the life problems and legal problems they are currently experiencing. If they continue to deny the problems with alcohol and drugs after being presented with evidence from their history that they have alcohol and drug-related problems, they may not be appropriate for a relapse prevention therapy at this time. It is recommended that they complete exercises 2, 3, and 4 and then be given the Alcohol and Drug Addiction Test again.

If after completing these exercises they are still not convinced that they are chemically dependent and need to totally abstain from alcohol and drugs, they should not continue with this workbook. Instead, they should enter a primary recovery program that focuses on three areas: (1) in-depth assessment of the recovering offender's alcohol and drug-use history and the current symptoms of chemical abuse and dependency; (2) interrupting the denial and addictive preoccupation by showing recovering offenders the causal connection between their chemical use and life problems; and (3) motivating recovering offenders to pursue a sober lifestyle based on abstinence from alcohol and other mood-altering drugs while pursuing a structured recovery program.

If the recovering offender does not show any signs of abuse or addiction, he or she should be referred for nonaddiction-focused counseling.

### Exercise #2: The Offender Personality Self-Test

The Offender Personality Self-Test was developed to help offenders identify the symptoms of antisocial personality disorder (ASPD). This twenty-two-item questionnaire was adapted from the DSM-IIIR criteria for ASPD. The symptoms were rewritten in language that recovering offenders could easily understand. A positive score on this test indicates the need for a diagnostic evaluation by a psychologist to confirm the diagnosis. This test is helpful to get offenders thinking about their antisocial behavior and its consequences, but it is not sufficient by itself to diagnose antisocial personality disorders.

It is recommended that the issue of antisocial or criminal personality traits be approached directly and nonjudgmentally with the offender. Offenders need to know the following:

- There is an illness called a criminal or antisocial personality.
- The symptoms of antisocial personality can be easily assessed.
- If people have a number of the symptoms, they have antisocial or criminal personality traits.
- These traits will cause irrational thinking and self-defeating behaviors that will cause people to continue to commit antisocial and criminal acts despite the adverse consequences.
- These traits will not go away by themselves.
- Treatment in the form of long-term counseling and therapy is necessary to change these antisocial traits.
- Most offenders who refuse to cooperate with treatment generally continue to act out in antisocial ways until they either get incarcerated for the rest of their lives, get killed or crippled while committing antisocial acts, or commit suicide in moments of severe depression.

Recovering offenders should complete the Offender Personality Self-Test and discuss the results with their individual counselor and in group therapy. Offenders should be asked if they agree with the results. If they do, why, and if not, why not? It is important to explore the thoughts and feelings the offenders have as they think about and talk about the test results. They normally experience an inner battle. One part of them believes they have a criminal personality and need to get well. Another part of them denies that they have a problem and blames their criminal behavior on others. If offenders can recognize and discuss both sides of this battle, they can begin to separate the sober and responsible part of their personality from the addictive and criminal part. They can then learn how to challenge addictive and criminal thinking and strengthen the sober and responsible thinking.

### Exercise #3: Why Do I Want to Change?

In this exercise, offenders are asked to describe why they want to get involved in treatment. It is important to recognize that there is usually a battle going on inside the offender. Part of them knows that they have a serious problem with alcohol, drugs, and criminal behavior and want to get well. This is the sober and responsible part of their personality. Another part, however, denies, rationalizes, and blames the problems on others. This part of the personality argues that they are social drinkers and recreational drug users who are being treated unfairly: "I don't need help! Other people should leave me alone, get off my back, and everything will be fine."

By getting recovering offenders to discuss openly why they want to be in treatment, the skillful counselor can help bring out both sides of this argument and continue to reinforce sober and responsible thinking while challenging addictive and criminal thinking.

Ask clients to complete this exercise by writing out why they have decided to enter a treatment program to help them to stop using alcohol, drugs, and criminal behaviors. When they present their reasons to the group, encourage the group to probe their true motivations. Do they really believe they have a serious problem with alcohol, or do they consider themselves social drinkers? Do they think of themselves as drug addicts or recreational drug users? Do they believe their criminal and antisocial behaviors are bad for them, or are they still blaming the victims and the enforcers who caught them?

If recovering offenders are just trying to get out of their current situation, have the group ask what they have tried before to get out of different problems and how that has worked. Try to have the group ask questions that clearly point out that recovering offenders must have commitment to long-term abstinence and a recovery program to successfully stay out of trouble.

### Exercise #4: Life, Addiction, and Criminal History

The Life, Addiction, and Criminal History is a critical exercise. The purpose of this exercise is to get the offender to carefully think through the sequence of life events that contributed to his or her use of alcohol, drugs, and criminal behaviors. The procedure divides the offender's life into eight areas: early childhood, grammar school, high school, college, military, adult work history, adult family and intimate history, and adult social and friendship history.

In each of these areas, the history questionnaire asks the offender to describe what that particular stage of his or her life was like and then specifically asks how alcohol and drug use and criminal behaviors affected that stage of life. The questionnaire is based on the belief that most chemically dependent criminal offenders never take the time to think through their entire life history. As a result, they cannot see the patterns that are getting them in trouble. Because they don't think about the sequence of the events they have experienced and how they have managed or mismanaged those events, they cannot learn from the past. Because they are incapable of learning from the past, they keep repeating self-defeating lifestyle patterns that lead them back to the use of alcohol, drugs, and criminal behaviors.

Most chemically dependent offenders use alcohol and drugs or engage in criminal or sexual thrill seeking to set off painful memories from the past. Most have been physically or sexually abused as children or adults. Many have suffered numerous injuries and traumas. As offenders begin reconstructing their histories, they often start to remember painful

177

events. These events reactivate their desire to escape by using alcohol, drugs, and criminal behaviors.

As a result, it is important to go slowly in processing the history and be alert for any signs of relapse that could be activated by the material in the history. If time permits, it is recommended that the client spend eight group sessions telling the story of his or her life and how it has been affected by alcohol and drugs. In the first group the client describes his or her early childhood. In the second group, grammar school experiences. In the third group, high school experiences. In the fourth group, college experiences (if applicable). In the fifth group, military experiences (if applicable). In the sixth group, adult work history. In the seventh group, adult intimate and family history. And, in the eighth group, adult social and friendship history.

This detailed life history review will do several things. First, it will allow the group leader and other group members to get a thorough and in-depth knowledge of each other. This promotes an emotional bonding among group members and begins addressing the isolation and inability to bond often seen in chemically dependent offenders. It also forces the offender to connect with unfinished emotional experiences from previous periods in life. These memories will bring intense feelings to the surface and often cause the offender to have catharsis experiences that lower stress and bring about emotional relief. By encouraging offenders to describe each area of life and then specifically discuss how alcohol and drug use and criminal behaviors affected that life area, they begin developing an in-depth understanding of the role their use of alcohol, drug use, and criminal behavior played in shaping the course of their lives.

There is a series of questions asked about each life area. The first question is: *What did the use of alcohol, drugs, and criminal behavior allow you to do or be in this area of life that you believed you couldn't do or be without it?* This question focuses on the irrational and magical expectations that alcohol, drugs, and criminal behaviors can somehow fix offenders or change important parts of their lives. Once these areas are exposed, the offender is usually more open to learning other ways to accomplish these things with sober and responsible behaviors.

The second question is: *What did the use of alcohol, drugs, and criminal behavior allow you to stop doing or being or allow you to escape from in this area of life that you felt trapped by without it?* This question focuses on the pain and problems in life that the offender attempted to escape from by using alcohol, drugs, and criminal behavior. Once this is exposed, the offender is more open to learning other ways to deal with these problems.

The third question is: *What benefits did you actually receive in this area of your life by using alcohol, drugs, and criminal behaviors?* This question acknowledges the reality that addiction and criminality do have some benefits. They provide a quick fix and make the offender temporarily feel good by blocking out pain and painful memories. They also provide a self-identity and give the offender ways to excuse or justify his or her behavior. In processing this question, it is important to show the offender that there are other ways to receive the same or similar benefits.

The fourth question is: *What problems did your use of alcohol, drugs, and criminal behaviors cause in this area of your life?* This question focuses on the progression of increasingly more severe problems that the offender experienced. It is important to let the offender know that there is hope and that recovery is possible. By following a recovery program, this progression of problems can be stopped and they can begin to build a meaningful and satisfying life based on principles of sobriety and responsibility.

In the final part of this exercise, offenders are asked to identify the reasons why they relapse. These questions are designed to evaluate if offenders are in the transition stage of DMR because they are still in strong denial and resistant to the idea of needing treatment; if they are in stabilization and cannot get back in control of their thoughts, feelings, and behaviors; or if they are in early recovery and want to live a sober, responsible life but simply don't know how to do it.

At the end of this exercise both the counselor and the offender should be able to clearly understand the repetitive sequence of life events that caused the development of progressively more severe life problems. The role of alcohol, drugs, and criminal behaviors in the development of those problems should be clearly established. The need to abstain from alcohol, drugs, and criminal behaviors and participate in a recovery program should be very clear.

### Exercise #5: The Relapse Calendar

The Relapse Calendar is a visual method for helping offenders summarize their past experiences with recovery and relapse. The calendar itself is a single page divided into thirteen columns. The first column is a space to enter the year, and the next twelve columns represent the twelve months of the year. The line for each year is divided into two parts: alcohol and drug use (A/D) and Legal. Offenders are asked to identify the month and year when they made their first serious attempt to stop using alcohol and drugs or criminal behaviors. Periods of abstinence are marked with a straight line, and periods of relapse are marked with jagged line.

The Relapse Calendar allows offenders to clearly see their pattern of recovery and relapse to both alcohol and drugs and criminal behaviors. By charting them both together, offenders are forced to see how relapsing to alcohol and drugs leads them back into criminal behavior and how relapsing into criminal behavior leads them back into alcohol and drug use. In processing the calendar, the counselor and the group should focus on this process of reciprocal relapse and reinforce the need for total abstinence from alcohol, drugs, and criminal behavior.

The Relapse Calendar should be processed in an individual counseling session and in group. Ask the recovering offenders to tell the story of their calendar in group. Some therapists have the offenders draw their calendar on a large sheet of paper or a blackboard so they can show the calendar to the group while they tell their story of recovery and relapse to the group.

## Exercise #6: The Relapse Episode List for Alcohol and Drugs

This exercise asks offenders to analyze their three most recent relapse episodes in more detail. They are asked to describe why they decided to stop using alcohol and drugs and the things they did to help stay clean and sober. They are also asked to describe what caused them to return to alcohol and drug use, what they believed that alcohol and drug use would help to accomplish, and what happened after they started to use. This detailed description can help identify the patterns that occur during sobriety that lead them back to alcohol and drug use.

## Exercise #7: The Relapse Episode List for Criminal Behavior

This is similar to exercise #6 except the focus is on criminal behaviors instead of alcohol and drug use. The same sequence of questions is asked and the offenders should be able to identify the patterns that occurred in recovery that led them back into the use of criminal behaviors.

## *The Outcome of Self-Assessment*

If the self-assessment exercises have been successful, recovering offenders should have a change in thinking based on their understanding that there is a relationship between the use of alcohol, drugs, and criminal behaviors. They should see that they need to abstain totally from all three if they want to recover. They should recognize that there is a powerful relationship between relapsing to alcohol and drugs and relapsing to criminal behaviors, and that they must recover from both chemical dependency and antisocial personality traits. Offenders should begin to get a picture that their past relapses have not been random events. They should begin to see that there are warning signs that set them up to relapse.

Emotionally, the recovering offenders should have connected with some deep unfinished emotional experiences from childhood and previous stages of life. They should have connected with pain and anger and have begun to experience some guilt or remorse about their past behaviors. They should be deeply unsettled but yet have a growing feeling of hope. Facing the pain and the problems should have created a catharsis that brought some emotional relief. By understanding their history, they should be hopeful that they can find a way out. Now the stage is set for warning sign identification.

## Section II: Warning Sign Identification

During this part of relapse prevention therapy, the recovering offenders review the common warning signs that lead from sober and responsible living back into the use of alcohol, drugs, and criminal behaviors. They review the lists and select the primary warning signs they identify with and carefully analyze each warning sign to find other hidden or unconscious problems that may lead to relapse. They then develop a comprehensive list of personal relapse warning signs. The five exercises completed during this part of relapse prevention therapy are:

### *Exercise #8 and #9: Relapse Warning Sign Review*

The purpose of this exercise is to give the recovering offenders detailed information about the relapse warning signs that lead them from a sober, responsible lifestyle back into the use of alcohol, drug, and criminal behaviors. The recovering offender is asked to review two lists of relapse warning signs. The first list, Relapse Warning Signs for Criminal Behavior, was developed primarily for offenders with criminal personality traits who also abuse alcohol and drugs. The second list, Relapse Warning Signs for Chemical Dependency, was develop primarily for chemically dependent people who do not have severe criminal personality traits but may tend to commit criminal acts to support their addiction.

Tell the recovering offenders that these relapse warning sign lists will help them understand how they return to the use of alcohol, drugs, and criminal behavior even though they don't want to. Explain that these lists describe the thoughts, feelings, and actions that offenders often experience before returning to alcohol or drug use or committing a crime.

Ask the recovering offenders to read both lists carefully. As they are reading the list they should: (1) put a check mark [√] next to any warning sign they have experienced; (2) put a question mark [?] next to any warning sign they have difficulty understanding; or (3) put an asterisk [*] next to any warning sign that causes them to "space out" or to start daydreaming while they are reading it.

The warning sign list can be reviewed by using one of three methods: the private reading method, the individual review method, and the group review method.

The **private reading method** involves asking the recovering offenders to read the list privately and discuss what they learned in group or individual counseling. Many chemically dependent offenders have difficulty reading and writing. As a result, they don't do very well when asked to read the warning sign lists by themselves as a homework assignment. This problem can be corrected by asking them to meet with another group member who has better reading skills to have them read and discuss the list together. Herald House/Independence Press has also published audiotapes of the warning signs being presented out loud. These tapes can be used by recovering offenders with literacy problems to privately review the warning signs.

Some counselors find it helpful to have the offenders read the warning sign list out loud in an individual counseling session, stopping to discuss warning signs of interest as they go along. This **individual review method** allows the offender to overcome problems caused by poor reading skills and to ask questions and discuss issues as they come up. Many counselors with large caseloads, however, do not have the time to do this.

A third possibility is to review the warning sign lists by reading them out loud and discussing them in a group session. This **group review method** is ideal for most criminal justice programs because up to ten or twelve offenders can review the warning signs at the same time in a supervised group. In very large groups, offenders should be divided into smaller groups of six to eight people. The group is told that they will spend the group session reading and commenting on one of the warning sign lists. One group member reads the first warning sign, the next group member reads the second warning sign, and so on with the reading assignments being passed around the group in a round-robin fashion. After the group has been reading the warning signs for about fifteen minutes, the reading stops and everyone in the group is asked to comment briefly (less than two minutes) about the warning signs that they identify with most. Then the group reads for another fifteen minutes and does another round of comments. The process continues until the entire list has been read.

It typically takes a ninety-minute group session for one of the lists to be reviewed. Many programs read and discuss the warning sign lists in a group as often as twice per week. Each time the list is read, different warning signs stand out to the group members. The discussion of warning signs usually brings up new and interesting information. The repetition reinforces understanding and memory of the warning signs. This is particularly helpful for offenders with literacy problems.

### *Exercise #10: The Initial Warning Sign List*

The primary goal of warning sign review is to give the recovering offenders new words to describe the problems that are leading them from stable recovery to relapse. These new words and ideas must be translated into a personal list of relapse warning signs. The recovering offenders must describe in their own words the sequence of problems that led them back to using alcohol, drugs, and criminal behaviors. The Initial Warning Sign List begins translating the warning signs from a professionally published version to a highly personalized version that matches the experiences of the individual recovering offender.

The initial warning sign list is developed by asking the recovering offenders to read the Relapse Warning Signs for Criminal Behavior and select the two warning signs on the list that most apply to them. They are asked to write out the title of both warning signs and describe why they selected each one. They are then asked to read the description of the warning signs again and underline the most important word or phrase

185

in each. They then describe what that word or phrase means to them.

Now they are ready to write a personalized warning sign title and a personalized warning sign description in their own words that will be easy for them to remember. It is important that the personalized description begin with the words, "I know I am in trouble with my recovery when...".

The recovering offender then repeats the same process using the Relapse Warning Signs for Chemical Dependency. In the end, the recovering offender will have an initial warning sign list that contains four personalized warning sign titles and descriptions. Two of these warning signs will be selected from the Relapse Warning Signs for Criminal Behavior and two will be selected from the Relapse Warning Signs for Chemical Dependency. The recovering offender will process this initial warning sign list in group or individual therapy.

### Exercise #11: Warning Sign Analysis Using the Card Sort Method

In this exercise, the recovering offenders analyze each of the warning signs on the Initial Warning Sign List. This analysis is designed to uncover hidden warning signs that contribute to relapse of which the recovering offender is unaware.

The process begins by asking the recovering offender to select the first warning sign on the Initial Warning Sign List that they would like to learn more about. They are then guided through three separate exercises to help them discover more information about that warning sign. These exercises are:

1. *Describing their personal reactions to the warning sign:* The offenders are asked to write down what they usually think, feel, have an urge to do, and actually do when they are experiencing this warning sign. They are also asked to describe what they start to do or say differently when experienc-

186

ing this warning sign that they don't do when not experiencing it, and what they stop doing or saying when experiencing this warning sign that they normally do when not experiencing it.

They are asked to read what they have written and look for hidden warning signs that are part of the description. They then write these new hidden warning signs in complete sentences in their own words on their warning sign identification cards. These cards provide a place on the front to write a personal title and description of the warning sign. On the back of the card is a place to write the thoughts, feelings, and actions that generally accompany the warning signs. These warning sign cards allow the offender to create a warning sign list by sorting the cards. It eliminates the need to write and rewrite lengthy lists as the order of the warning signs is rearranged.

Recovering offenders are instructed to use one card for each new hidden warning sign. They write a brief title (a word or a short phrase) for each new hidden warning sign that tells them what the warning sign is about. The purpose of the title is to give them an easy way to remember what the warning sign is and to tell others about it quickly and easily. They are then asked to write a one-sentence description for each hidden warning sign that begins with the words, "I know I am in trouble with my recovery when...". This description tells what happens when they act out the warning sign.

For personal warning signs to be effective, the way the warning sign is written must "feel right" to the recovering offenders. To make sure it feels right, ask the offenders to take a deep breath and read the sentence out loud several times. If it doesn't feel right when read aloud, different words should be used until it does.

At the end of analyzing the description, the recovering offenders may have discovered from five to fifteen hidden warning signs written on individual cards. They should arrange the cards in the order the warning signs generally occur. They do this by reading the first card and putting it down in front of them. Then they read the second card and ask themselves if this usually happens before or after the first card, and they put the second card either before or after the first card. They then read the third card and ask if that occurs before, in the middle, or after the first two cards, and they put it in the proper position. They continue to place each new card in the correct order. If they notice that two cards say almost the same thing, one of them is discarded. They are then ready to move on to the next part of the exercise.

2. *Describing a past experience with the warning sign:* The recovering offenders are asked to describe in writing a specific past experience when they experienced this warning sign while sober. As they describe the situation they are asked to make sure to answer the questions who, what, when, and where: Who were you with when the warning sign was triggered? What were you doing? What was going on around you? When did this happen? Where did this happen?

It is important to capture the specific sequence of events that occurred after the warning sign was triggered. Offenders can be asked to tell the past event like a story with a beginning, a middle, and an ending. They can also be asked: "When was the warning sign triggered? What was the first thing you did when it was triggered? The second thing? The third thing? What finally happened that brought the situation to an end?"

The offender is asked to read what has been written and look for hidden warning signs that are part of the description. These new hidden warning signs are written on new warning sign identification cards.

Once again the cards are arranged in order; the new cards are added to the previous cards and arranged in the correct sequence, and obvious duplications are eliminated.

3. *Describing a future experience with the warning sign:*

Now the recovering offenders move on to the third part of this exercise by describing a specific future experience when they believe they will experience this warning sign again while sober. Just as with the past description, they want to get an exact sequence of events that describes who, what, when, and where.

The offenders are asked to read the description of the future event and to look for hidden warning signs that are part of the description. They write these new hidden warning signs in complete sentences in their own words on the warning sign identification cards and, once again, arrange the cards in the order the warning signs generally occur while eliminating obvious duplications.

This warning sign analysis procedure is then completed again for the other two warning signs on the Initial Warning Sign List. The process takes time and a lot of work, but clinical experience indicates that it is by careful and probing analysis that the most powerful hidden warning signs that trigger relapse are identified and brought into conscious awareness. Without this rigorous analysis process, many powerful warning signs that trigger renewed use of alcohol, drugs, and criminal behaviors would be missed, leaving the offender vulnerable to relapse.

At the end of the warning sign analysis process, the recovering offender has a stack of between fifteen and forty loosely organized cards. The goal is to carefully organize this stack into a final warning sign list consisting of between ten and fifteen cards.

### Exercise #12: The Final Warning Sign List

The goal of creating a Final Warning Sign List is to help the recovering offender to write a clear and concise list of the situations, thoughts, feelings, and actions that leads him or her from stable, sober, and responsible living back to the use of alcohol, drugs, and criminal behaviors. There are a number of steps in turning the stack of cards developed by warning sign analysis into a first-rate and effective personalized warning sign list. These steps are:

*Exercise #12-A: Checking the Titles:* The recovering offender reads through the stack of warning sign identification cards and checks to be sure that each card has a title. The title should be a word or a short phrase that is easy to remember and that tells exactly what the warning sign is all about. The shorter, clearer, and easier to remember each title is, the better (correct any titles that need it).

*Exercise #12-B: Checking the Descriptions:* The recovering offenders read the stack of warning sign cards again. This time they pay special attention to each description statement, making sure the descriptions are clear by asking the following questions about each card: (1) Is the description a complete sentence? (2) Does the sentence describe them doing something or wanting to do something either by themselves or with or to someone or something else? (3) Are they the person who is doing the action in the warning sign? (What other people do or want to do are not personal warning signs. Offenders need to focus on their own thoughts, feelings, and reactions to what others do). (4) Did they use the same words in the title and the description? It is important to use different words in the title and the description.

*Exercise #12-C: Eliminating Duplications:* The recovering offenders read the warning sign cards again to see if there are any warning signs that say about the same thing. Sometimes two or more warning signs can be easily combined. Many warning sign cards contain thoughts, feelings, or action urges that can be merged with other cards. Remember, the goal is to end up with a final warning sign list of between twelve and eighteen warning sign cards. As the following exercises are completed, keep looking for warning signs that can be combined or eliminated.

*Exercise #12-D: Filling Out the Back of the Cards:* On the back of each card is a place for the recovering offenders to write a thought statement, a feeling statement, and an action statement. Starting with the first card they do the following:

*Step 1: Thought Statement:* They read the personal title and description and ask themselves, "What thoughts are usually going on in my head when I am experiencing this warning sign?" They pick the most important thought and write in the space next to the word *think* on the back of the card. A good thought statement starts with the words, "When I experience this warning sign I tend to think...".

*Step 2: Feeling Statement:* They read the personal title and the description again and ask themselves, "What am I usually feeling when I experience this relapse warning sign?" They read their thought statement out loud several times and ask themselves, "What kind of feelings will be caused by thinking this thought?" They write a feeling statement next to the word *feel* on the back of the card. A good feeling statement starts with the words, "When I experience this warning sign I tend to feel...". Use the following list of feeling words to help you describe your feelings:

---

### When I experience this warning sign I tend to feel...

- strong and powerful
- weak and helpless
- angry, mad, or resentful
- warm, caring, or protective
- happy or joyful
- sad, sorrowful, or depressed
- safe, secure, or complacent
- threatened, scared, or afraid
- stuck or frustrated
- satisfied, fulfilled, or bored
- ashamed or guilty

---

*Step 3: Action Urge Statement:* They then read the personal title and the description again and ask themselves, "What do

I usually have an urge to do when I experience this warning sign?" They read the thought and feeling statement several times out loud and ask themselves, "What are those thoughts and feelings likely to cause me to want to do about it?" They write an action statement next to the words *urge to* on the back of the cards. A good action statement starts with the words, "When I experience this warning sign I have an urge to...".

*Step 4: Read the Next Warning Sign Card:* The next warning sign card should describe an event that logically follows from the action urge statement. When we have an action urge we either try to ignore it or we act it out. Here's an example:

> *Title Of Warning Sign #1:* Trapped
> *Description:* I know that I am in trouble with my recovery when I start believing that being clean and sober is like being in jail because I can't do what I want to do.
> *When I experience this warning sign I tend to think:* I can't win, no matter what I do.
> *When I experience this warning sign I tend to feel:* depressed.
> *When I experience this warning sign I have an urge to:* go back into the old life in order to get my freedom back and to feel excited and alive.
> *Title of Warning Sign #2:* Old Friends
> *Description:* I know that I am in trouble with my recovery when I feel the urge to hang out with the people I used to drink, drug, and commit crimes with.

Notice, in the above example, how the thought creates the feeling, the feeling creates the action urge, and the action urge creates the next warning sign. As recovering offenders fill out the back of the cards they may find there are some gaps in the action that need new warning sign cards. They may find that some of the cards need to be rewritten or eliminated.

*Exercise #12-E: Filling in the Gaps in the Action*: This exercise will make sure that there are no warning signs missing in the personalized warning sign list. Missing warning signs are called gaps in the action.

The recovering offenders do the following: (1) They read both the front and the back of their warning sign identification cards and notice the sequence of events. (2) They try to see themselves moving through the sequence of events. They notice in their mind how they move from one warning sign to the next. (3) They ask themselves, "Are there any gaps in the action? Do I skip a step anywhere in the process?" (4) If they notice any gaps in the action, they write new warning signs cards that will fill in those gaps in the space below.

*Exercise #12-F: Backtracking to Earlier Warning Signs:* Recovering offenders normally don't start to notice that they are in trouble until things have already started to go wrong. This exercise helps them to think about where the problems with relapse really begin.

To backtrack to earlier warning signs, they do the following: (1) Look at the first warning sign card and ask, "Is this really where it started? What happened that caused this first warning sign to occur?" If they can think of an earlier warning sign, they write a new warning side card that describes it. (2) They read the new warning sign they just wrote and ask, "What happened that caused this warning sign to occur?" If they can think of an earlier warning sign, they write it on a new warning sign card. (3) They repeat this process until they can't think of any earlier warning signs.

*Exercise #12-G: Relapse Justifications:* This exercise helps recovering offenders think about how they persuade themselves to start using alcohol, drugs, and criminal behaviors.

They look at the last two or three warning signs on their list and ask, "Do these warning signs describe the last things that happened to me before I started using alcohol, drugs, or criminal behaviors? Are there any other thoughts, feelings, people, or situations that I used as an excuse to justify in my mind going back to using alcohol, drugs, or criminal behaviors?" Be sure that the offenders have at least two warning sign cards that describe how they convince themselves it is a good idea or have no other choice but to start using alcohol, drugs or criminal behaviors.

Another way to do this is to ask the offender to stack the cards from beginning to end and then ask, "Where in this sequence of events do I first start to think about using alcohol and drugs? Where in this sequence of events do I first start to think about using criminal behaviors?"

*Exercise #12-H: Final Warning Sign List:* This exercise will help recovering offenders fill in anything that was missing in their Initial Warning Sign List. By this time the offenders may be frustrated because they have to write the list again, but encourage them to keep at it. Writing the list again is very important to come up with a complete warning sign list.

Ask the recovering offender to read you his or her warning sign cards one more time. Be sure any new warning sign cards have been placed in the correct order. It must be clear how one warning sign causes the next one to occur. The first warning sign happens, then they think self-defeating thoughts that cause them to have unmanageable feelings that create the urge to act out the next warning sign.

Here is an example of how it works:

*Title of Warning Sign #1:* Got to Have It My Way
*Description:* I know I am in trouble with my recovery when I believe I have to have everything go the way I want it to whether I am right or not.
*When this happens I tend to think:* I am right and you are wrong! I can't do anything wrong!

194

*When I think these thoughts I tend to feel:* powerful and strong.

*When I feel this way I have an urge to:* push other people around and tell them what to do.

*Title of Warning Sign #2:* Pushing Others Around

*Description:* I know I am in trouble with my recovery when I begin acting like a bully and forcing people to do things my way by manipulating and threatening them.

*When this happens I tend to think:* other people are dumb and stupid and need me to tell them what to do.

*When I think these thoughts I tend to feel:* angry at others, powerful.

*When I have these feelings I have an urge to:* get away from these dumb people who make so much trouble for me.

*Title of Warning Sign #3:* Being Alone

## Section III: Warning Sign Management

During this part of relapse prevention therapy clients complete a series of structured exercises that shows them how to select critical warning signs and develop new ways of coping with those warning signs by changing their way of thinking, managing their feeling and emotions, and acting. The four exercises completed during this part of relapse prevention therapy are:

### *Exercise # 13: Identifying and Managing Critical Warning Signs*

The purpose of this two-part exercise is to help the recovering offenders 'select the key or critical warning signs that lead them from sober, responsible living back into the use of alcohol, drugs, and criminal behaviors and to develop new strategies for coping with them that could stop the progression of warning signs and get them back into a stable recovery.

Critical warning signs meet three criteria: (1) the recovering offender will easily recognize a critical warning sign even if he or she is upset or angry; (2) critical warning signs will occur early enough for the recovering offender to take positive action to intervene; and (3) the recovering offender will be motivated to deal with the critical warning sign in order to avoid relapse.

The first step is to review the Final Warning Sign List and identify three warning signs that meet the criteria. Each of these warning signs is written at the top of a blank sheet of paper and with a description of why it is a critical warning sign.

The next step is to develop a plan for managing the critical warning signs. This is done by writing out the story of a past situation in which the critical warning sign was mismanaged. It is important for the offender to describe the sequence of irrational thoughts, unmanageable feelings, and self-defeating behaviors that began once the warning sign was activated.

The next step is to identify three **intervention points** in this older sequence of events where the offender could have done something different to produce a better outcome. One intervention point should be near the beginning, one near the middle, and one near the end of the situation. Offenders then describe how they could act differently at each intervention point and how this different behavior would produce a better outcome. This should result in three concrete plans for managing each of the three critical warning signs more effectively should it develop.

## Exercise #14: Managing the Thoughts that Lead to Relapse

Relapsing into the use of alcohol, drugs, and criminal behavior is often caused by the way recovering offenders think. In this exercise they will learn how to identify three primary irrational thoughts that lead them from sober, responsible living back into the use of alcohol, drugs, and criminal behaviors. They will then learn more effective ways of thinking that can prevent relapse.

To do this the offenders review the three critical warning signs they previously identified. They read the thought statements they wrote on the back of the warning sign cards. They write each thought on the top of a separate sheet of paper. Underneath each thought they describe how that thought sets them up to relapse.

The next step is to identify the **mandate** that goes along with the irrational thought. A mandate is a specific way of thinking that tells the offenders that they *must, should,* or *have to* do something or something awful will happen. To identify the mandate associated with each irrational thought, ask the offenders to read the irrational thought out loud and ask themselves, "What does this irrational thought tell me I must do?"

This mandate threatens a consequence by telling the offenders that if they don't do what the mandate tells them, they must do something negative or something awful will happen. To identify the threatened consequence, ask the offenders to read the mandate out loud and ask themselves, "What do I believe is going to happen if I don't do what the mandate tells me I must do?" Write this consequence statement right after the mandate.

The next step is to identify the **injunction** that goes along with the irrational thought. An injunction is a specific way of thinking that tells the offenders that they *must not, should not,* or *cannot* do something. To identify the injunction associated with each irrational thought, ask the offenders to read the irrational thought out loud and ask, "What does this irrational thought tell me I must not do?" Write down the injunction.

This injunction threatens a consequence by telling the offenders that, if they do what the injunction tells them they must not do, something negative or awful will happen. To identify the threatened consequence, ask the offenders to read the injunction and ask themselves the question, "What is this injunction telling me is going to happen if I do what the injunction is telling me I must not do?" Write this consequence statement right after the injunction.

The next step is to challenge the **source of authority** by identifying the people who first taught the offenders they must or can't think, feel, or do these things. Once the source of authority is identified, challenge the offenders by asking them if it is possible that this authority figure was wrong. All sources of authority are ultimately fallible human beings capable of mistakes. Is it possible this authority made a mistake by teaching this mandate and injunction?

The next step is to have the offenders write down the **benefits and disadvantages** of continuing to believe the mandates and injunctions are true, and the benefits and disadvantages of challenging the mandates and injunctions and starting to think differently.

Finally, the offenders are asked to identify another way of thinking that will allow them a **choice** between a sober, responsible response and an addictive or criminal response when this mandate and injunction are activated.

## Exercise #15: Managing Feelings that Lead to Relapse

Relapsing into the use of alcohol, drugs, and criminal behavior is often caused by the way recovering offenders manage their feelings. In this exercise recovering offenders learn how to identify three primary feelings that they mismanaged in a way that led them from sober, responsible living back into the use of alcohol, drugs, and criminal behaviors.

The offenders will then learn more effective ways of managing those feelings that can prevent relapse.

To do this recovering offenders review the three critical warning signs that they previously identified and read the feelings that are written on the back of the warning sign cards. They write each of these unmanageable feelings at the top of a blank sheet of paper. Underneath each feeling they answer three questions:

1. What sensation do I have in my body when I am experiencing this feeling? (This will help the offenders recognize the feeling in the future when they have it.)

2. How have I mismanaged this feeling in the past that led to relapse? (Here the counselor educates and probes for one of two classic patterns of emotional mismanagement: stuffing the feeling, building up like a pressure, exploding, acting out, and feeling guilty; or emotionally overreacting, converting the emotion to anger, acting out against others, and blaming and resenting the victim.)

3. What is a new, more effective way of managing this feeling to avoid relapse? (Here the counselor educates about the steps of effective emotional management which include recognizing an inner feeling, accurately labeling it with a feeling word, and communicating it to others in a safe and supportive environment.)

## Exercise #16: Managing Behaviors that Lead to Relapse

Relapsing into the use of alcohol, drugs, and criminal behavior is often caused by the way recovering offenders behave or act. In this exercise offenders learn how to identify the three primary action urges and behaviors that lead from sober, responsible living back into the use of alcohol, drugs, and criminal behaviors. They then learn more effective ways of acting that can prevent relapse.

199

To do this the recovering offenders review the three critical warning signs and read the action urges that they previously wrote on the back of their warning sign cards. They write each of these action urges on a separate sheet of paper. Next they identify the **triggering event** by describing the situation or event that creates the urge for them to use this self-defeating behavior. Then they describe the **action urge** by describing exactly what they feel an urge to do when the trigger goes off.

Then they describe what their **actual behavior** was, which is what they actually do when the trigger goes off. Some people have an urge to do one thing but repress the urge and do something else. Other people lack impulse control and feel they have to do something simply because they feel the urge to do it. Finally, offenders are asked to identify **more effective behaviors** that they could do instead of the self-defeating behavior.

## Section IV: Recovery Planning

After recovering offenders have identified the critical warning signs that lead from sober, responsible living back to the use of alcohol, drugs, and criminal behavior, it is time for them to develop a schedule of recovery activities that can assist them in identifying and managing the critical warning signs.

Recovery is like walking up a down escalator. There is no such thing as standing still. The recovering offenders will need to work every day at identifying their relapse warning signs and the thoughts, feelings, and actions that drive them. They must constantly put themselves in situations that will support sobriety and responsible living. They must consciously use new ways of thinking, managing their feelings, and acting when they are in those situations.

Initially this will be hard for them to do because their addictive and criminal habits have been so deeply ingrained in their personality. Without a daily schedule of recovery activities, they will relapse into old ways of thinking, managing their feelings, acting, and relating to others. This will lead them to get involved in addiction and crime-centered situations and eventually cause them to go back to alcohol, drugs, and crime.

If recovering offenders consistently practice the new ways of thinking, feeling, and acting by following their recovery program, the new behaviors will begin to feel comfortable. After four to six weeks of consistently following the program, most of these activities become unconscious habits that are easy to maintain. Because these new habits are effective, the recovering offender's life becomes more manageable and the ability to feel good in life increases.

The following exercises will help the recovering offenders understand what recovery activities are helpful to them. It will then help them to develop an initial recovery plan, test it to be sure it deals with their critical warning signs, and revise and strengthen it so it can be effective in preventing relapse.

### Exercise #17-A: Recovery Activities

Having a plan for each day will help offenders stay away from alcohol, drugs, and criminal behavior. People who successfully recover tend to do certain basic things. In AA there is such a strong belief that they work that many people with solid recovery will say, "If you want what we have, do what we did!" and "It works if you work it!"

Not everyone in recovery, however, does exactly the same things. Once recovering offenders develop a basic understanding of themselves and the basic principles of recovery, they can build an effective personal program.

When recovering offenders first read the following list they tend to get defensive. "I can't do all of those things," they say to themselves. At this point it is helpful to invite the recovering offenders to think about their recovery as if they were hiking in the Grand Canyon and had to jump across a ravine that is about three feet wide and a hundred feet deep. It is better to jump three feet too far than risk jumping one inch to short. The same is true of recovery. It is better to plan to do a little bit more than you need to do than to risk not doing enough. In AA they say, "Half measures availed us nothing!"

The seven basic recovery activities described below are actually habits of good healthy living. Anyone who wants to live a responsible, healthy, and fulfilling life gets in the habit of regularly doing these things. For people in recovery from chemical dependency and criminal personality, these activities are essential. A regular schedule of these activities, designed to match their unique profile of recovery needs and relapse warning signs, is necessary for the brain to heal from the damage caused by chronic alcohol and drug poisoning and for the personality to change.

The following list describes the basic recovery activities that successfully recovering people have described as most helpful to their recovery. Ask the recovering offenders to read this list and identify which activities they think would be helpful in their recovery, the obstacles they face in doing these activities on a regular basis, and their willingness to overcome those obstacles.

(1) *Professional Counseling:* Successful recovery depends on regular attendance at recovery education sessions, group therapy sessions, and individual therapy sessions. The scientific literature on treatment effectiveness clearly shows that the more time recovering people invest in professional counseling and therapy during the first two years of recovery, the more likely they are to stay sober, live responsibly, and avoid renewed criminal behavior.

(2) *Self-help Programs:* There are a number of self-help programs such as Alcoholics Anonymous (AA), Narcotics

Anonymous (NA), and Rational Recovery that can support offenders in their efforts to live sober and responsible lives. These programs all have several things in common: (1) they ask recovering offenders to abstain from alcohol and drugs and live a responsible and crime-free life; (2) they encourage recovering offenders to attend meetings regularly so they can meet and develop relationships with other people living sober and responsible lives; (3) they ask recovering offenders to meet regularly with an established member of the group (usually called a sponsor) who will help them learn about the organization and get through the rough spots; and (4) they promote a program of recovery (often in the form of steps or structured exercises that are worked on outside of meetings) that focuses on techniques for changing thinking, managing emotions, and altering behavior. Scientific research shows that the more committed and actively involved recovering people are in self-help groups during the first two years of recovery, the greater the chance of avoiding relapse.

*3. Proper Diet:* What recovering people eat can affect how they think, feel, and act. Many chemically dependent people find that they feel better if they eat three well-balanced meals per day, use vitamin and amino acid supplements, avoid eating sugar and foods made with white flower, and cut back or stop smoking cigarettes and drinking caffeinated beverages such as coffee and colas. Recovering people who don't follow these simple principles of healthy diet and meal planning tend to feel anxious and depressed, have strong and violent mood swings, feel chemically angry and resentful, periodically experience powerful cravings, and are more likely to relapse. Those who follow a proper diet feel better and have lower relapse rates.

*4) Exercise Program:* Doing thirty minutes of aerobic exercise each day will help the brain of recovering people to heal and allow them to feel better about themselves. Fast walking, jogging, swimming, or aerobics classes are all helpful. It is also helpful to do strength-building exercises (such as weight lifting) and flexibility exercises (such as stretching) in addition to the aerobic exercise.

(5.) *Stress Management Program:* Stress is a major cause of relapse. Recovering people who learn how to manage stress without using alcohol, drugs, or criminal behaviors stay clean and sober. Those who don't learn to manage stress relapse. Stress management involves learning relaxation exercises and taking quiet time on a daily basis to relax. It also involves avoiding long hours of working and taking time for recreation and relaxation.

(6.) *Spiritual Development Program:* Human beings have both a physical self (based on the health of our brains and body) and a nonphysical self (based on the health of our value system and spiritual lives). Most recovering people find that they need to invest regular time in developing themselves spiritually (in other words, exercising the nonphysical aspects of who they are).

Twelve Step programs such as AA provide an excellent program for spiritual recovery as do many churches and spiritual programs. At the heart of any spiritual program are three activities: (1) fellowship, during which people spend time talking with other people using similar methods; (2) private prayer and meditation, during which people take time alone to pray and meditate and to consciously put themselves in the presence of a higher power or to consciously reflect on the spiritual self; and (3) group worship, during which people pray and meditate with other people sharing a similar spiritual philosophy.

(7.) *Morning and Evening Inventories:* People who avoid relapse and successfully recover learn how to break free of automatic and unconscious addictive and criminal responses. They learn to live consciously each day, being aware of what they are doing, and taking responsibility for what they do and the consequences. To stay consciously aware they take time each morning to plan their day (Morning Planning Inventory) and they take time each evening to review their progress and problems (Evening Review Inventory). They discuss what they learn about themselves with other people who are involved in their recovery program.

### Exercise #17-B: The Initial Recovery Plan

After reading the list of standard recovery activities, the recovering offender is asked to think of a typical week and write a recovery plan. A good recovery plan consists of: (1) the day and time of each scheduled recovery activity (it is helpful to have two or three recovery activities scheduled for each day); and (2) the primary relapse prevention goal of each recovery activity.

### Exercise #17-C: Testing the Recovery Plan

The first recovery plans offenders write usually look good but fail to include recovery activities specifically designed to help identify and manage their critical warning signs. To correct this problem the offenders take a sheet of paper and divide it into two columns. In the first column they list the titles of their relapse warning signs by copying them in the correct order from their Final Warning Sign List. In the second column, they list all recovery activities from their initial recovery plan that have the primary focus of helping them to identify and manage that warning sign. Be sure to list only recovery activities that directly relate to the identification and management of the warning sign (for example, AA attendance does not address the identification or management of a warning sign titled "Arguments with Spouse"). This exercise will expose the weaknesses in the recovery plan.

## Exercise 17-D: Final Recovery Plan

Now the recovering offenders are ready to construct a Final Recovery Plan that addresses the weaknesses that they discovered in the initial recovery plan by systematically comparing it to the warning sign list. They do this by writing a new schedule of daily recovering activities.

## Exercise #18: Morning and Evening Inventories

The first steps in learning to avoid relapse are: (1) identifying the relapse warning signs, (2) developing management strategies for critical warning signs, and (3) developing a recovery program that will support the ongoing identification and management of relapse warning signs.

Warning signs often develop unconsciously. In other words, recovering offenders can experience warning signs and not know it because they are so involved in other things. By using daily inventories they can train themselves to become aware of warning signs as they develop and to make conscious decisions to use their warning sign management strategies.

The most effective inventory method is to conduct a planning inventory every morning and a review inventory every evening. The Morning Planning Inventory takes about fifteen minutes each morning. It helps recovering offenders plan the day, schedule their recovery activities, and stay aware of the warning signs that they may experience.

The Morning Planning Inventory includes goals for the day, the recovery activities that need to be completed that day, and other daily tasks. The recovery activities and daily tasks are entered on a time schedule to assure that there is sufficient time to complete them.

The Evening Review Inventory takes about fifteen minutes each evening. It gives recovering offenders the opportunity to review the activities of their day, evaluate if they successfully

206

completed their recovery activities and other daily tasks, and notice if they experienced any relapse warning signs. It also gives them a chance to decide if they need help or support in dealing with what happened during the day.

These daily morning and evening inventories are vital exercises that help recovering offenders stay consciously aware of their progress and to promptly identify and take corrective actions should warning signs develop.

# A Final Word

Chemically dependent criminal offenders suffer from both chemical dependency and criminal personality disorders. With proper diagnosis and treatment they can recover. Relapse prevention therapy can be a vital tool in helping recovering offenders avoid relapsing to the use of alcohol, drugs, and criminal behaviors.

Guiding recovering offenders through the relapse prevention therapy process will help them to identify personal relapse warning signs, discover the weaknesses in their past recovery program that made them vulnerable to relapse, and develop new ways to identify and manage their relapse warning signs without the use of alcohol, drugs, or criminal behaviors.

The professional relationship you develop with recovering offenders is critical to motivating them to develop a sober, responsible lifestyle. You can show them that they need to make a firm decision to stop using alcohol, drugs, and criminal behavior. You can challenge them to give up their old ways of thinking, feeling, and acting so they can have a better life. You can help them put what they have learned into action by completing this workbook.

It is important to constantly reinforce that the offender needs to keep learning, growing, and changing. Many people whose lives were previously destroyed by chemical addiction and criminal behaviors have recovered and are living happy, productive lives. It is your job to empower the offender to believe that he or she can recover and reclaim his or her life.

Relapse prevention planning is never really over. Chemically dependent criminal offenders have two serious problems that have a tendency toward relapse. The first problem is chemical dependency marked by deeply entrenched habits of addictive thinking. The second problem is criminal personality traits marked by deeply entrenched habits of criminal and antisocial thinking. Just because recovering offenders have temporarily broken out of these destructive patterns doesn't guarantee their long-term success. There is a rule to recovery: people are either growing or they are dying; they are either recovering or setting themselves up for relapse. Recovering people must make a conscious choice about which path they will follow each day.

Relapse prevention therapy does not guarantee lifelong recovery, but it does increase the offender's power of choice. Once recovering offenders identify their early relapse warning signs, they can choose to take action to manage them before they grow into an uncontrollable nightmare that drives them back to addictive use.

It is important to remember that chemically dependent criminal offenders can and do recover. They are difficult to treat, but they are not impossible to treat. Relapse prevention therapy, when used as an integrated part of a comprehensive structured recovery program, can increase the chances of long-term recovery for many offenders who have previously relapsed after treatment.

Your efforts can and do make a difference. Good luck in your ongoing efforts to help chemically dependent criminal offenders recover and avoid relapse.

# Bibliography and Suggested Readings

American Psychiatric Association. *Diagnostic and Statistical Manual of Mental Disorders*, 3rd ed., rev. Washington, D.C.: American Psychiatric Association, 1987.

Beck, Aaron T., and Arthur Freeman. *Cognitive Therapy of Personality Disorders*. New York, London: Guilford Press, 1990.

Brown, Stephanie. *Treating the Alcoholic: A Developmental Model of Recovery*. New York: John Wiley & Sons, 1985.

Cadoret, Remi J., Ed Troughton, and Thomas W. Gorman. "Genetic and Environmental Factors in Alcohol Abuse and Antisocial Personality," *Journal of Studies on Alcohol* 48, no. 1 (1987): 1-8.

Downing, Cynthia. *Surrender to Powerlessness and Its Relationship to Relapse in Recovering Alcoholics*. Published dissertation, Saybrook Institute, California, 1991.

Ewing, J. A. "Detecting Alcoholism, The CAGE Questionnaire," *Journal of the American Medical Association* 252 (1984): 1905-1907.

Forrest, Gary G. *Chemical Dependency and Antisocial Personality Disorder, Volume 1: Epidemiology, Etiology, and Differential Diagnosis*. New York, London, Sydney: Haworth Press, 1993.

_____. *Chemical Dependency and Antisocial Personality Disorder, Volume 2: Psychotherapy and Rehabilitation*. New York, London, Sydney: Haworth Press, 1993.

Gillen R., and V. Hesselbrock. "Cognitive Functioning, ASP, and Family History of Alcoholism in Young Men at Risk for Alcoholism," *Alcohol Clin. Exp. Res.* 16, no. 2 (1992): 206-214.

Glen, Susan Wagner, et al. "The Role of Antisocial, Affective, and Childhood Behavioral Characteristics in Alcoholics

Neuropsychological Performance," *Alcohol Clin. Exp. Res.* 17, no. 1 (1993): 162-169.

Gorski, Terence T., and Merlene Miller. *The Management of Aggression and Violence.* Homewood, Illinois: The CE-NAPS Corporation, 1981.

_____. *Counseling for Relapse Prevention.* Independence, Missouri: Herald House/Independence Press, 1982.

_____. *Staying Sober: A Guide for Relapse Prevention.* Independence, Missouri: Herald House/Independence Press, 1986.

Gorski, Terence T. *The Staying Sober Workbook: A Serious Solution for the Problem of Relapse.* Independence, Missouri: Herald House/Independence Press, 1988.

_____. *How to Start Relapse Prevention Support Groups.* Independence, Missouri: Herald House/Independence Press, 1989.

_____. *Passages Through Recovery: An Action Plan for Preventing Relapse.* Center City, Minnesota: Hazelden, 1989.

_____. *Understanding the Twelve Steps: A Guide for Counselors, Therapists, and Recovering People.* Independence, Missouri: Herald House/Independence Press, 1989.

_____. *Relapse Prevention Therapy with Chemically Dependent Criminal Offenders, Part 1: An Executive Briefing for Policy Makers and Judges.* Independence, Missouri: Herald House/Independence Press, 1994.

_____. *Relapse Prevention Therapy with Chemically Dependent Criminal Offenders, Part 3: The Relapse Prevention Workbook for the Criminal Offender.* Independence, Missouri: Herald House/Independence Press, 1994.

_____. *Getting Love Right: Learning the Choices of Healthy Intimacy.* New York: Fireside Press, 1993.

_____. *Treating the Chemically Dependent Criminal Offender.* Mental Health in Corrections Symposium, U.S. Department of Commerce, National Technical Information Services, 5285 Port Royal Road, Springfield, VA 22161, June 1993.

Helgoe, Robert S. *Recovery, A Pull from the Source: The Meaning and Measurement of Recovery from Alcoholism and Addictions.* Selah, Washington: Sundown M Foundation, 1989.

Mayfield, D. G., G. McLeod, and P. Hall. "The CAGE Questionnaire, Validation of a New Alcoholism Screening Instrument," *American Journal of Psychiatry* 131 (1974): 1121-1123.

Miller, Merlene, Terence T. Gorski, and David Miller. *Learning to Live Again: A Guide for Recovery from Chemical Dependency.* Independence, Missouri: Herald House/Independence Press, 1992.

Miller, Merlene, and Terence T. Gorski. *Staying Sober Recovery Education Modules: Exercise Manual.* Independence, Missouri: Herald House/Independence Press, 1989.

Millon, Theodore, and George S. Everly, Jr. *Personality and Its Disorders.* New York: John Wiley and Sons, 1985.

Selzer, M. L. "The Michigan Alcoholism Screening Test: The Quest for a New Diagnostic Instrument," *American Journal of Psychiatry* 127 (1971): 1653-1658.

Swensen, W. M., and R. M. Morris. "The Use of a Self-administered Alcoholism Screening Test (SAAST) in a Medical Center," *Mayo Clinic, Proc.* 50 (1975): 204-208.

U.S. Department of Health and Human Services. *Seventh Special Report to the U.S. Congress on Alcohol and Health.* Washington, D.C.: January 1990.

Walker, Robert. "Substance Abuse and B-Cluster Disorders I: Understanding The Dual Diagnosis Recovering Offender," *Journal of Psychoactive Drugs* 24, no. 3 (July-September 1992): 223-232.

_____. "Substance Abuse and B-Cluster Disorders II: Treatment Recommendations," *Journal of Psychoactive Drugs* 24, no. 3 (July-September 1992): 233-241.

Yochelson, Samuel, and Stanton E. Samenow. *The Criminal Personality, Volume 1: A Profile for Change*. Northvale, New Jersey, and London: Jason Aronson, 1976.

_____. *The Criminal Personality, Volume 2: The Change Process*. Northvale, New Jersey, and London: Jason Aronson, 1985.

_____. *The Criminal Personality, Volume 3: The Drug User*. Northvale, New Jersey, and London: Jason Aronson, 1986.

## Information Resources

National Clearinghouse for Alcohol and Drug Information (NCADI), 1-800-729-6686.

National Criminal Justice System Reference Service (NCJRS), 1-800-851-3420.

Drugs and Crime Data Center and Clearing House, 1-800-666-3322.

The CENAPS® Corporation, 6147 Deltona Blvd., Spring Hill, FL 34606, 352/596-8000.

Herald House/Independence Press, 1001 West Walnut, P.O. Box 390, Independence, MO 64051-0390: 1-800-767-8181 or 816/521-3015.

# Dictionary of Terms

**Abstinence:** The state of being free from the use of alcohol, other mood-altering drugs, criminal thinking, and criminal behaviors. Abstinence is a primary goal of recovery. Abstinence is the absence of use. The term sobriety means to live a healthy, effective life while abstinent. Sobriety, therefore, means abstinence plus meaningful and effective living.

**Addiction:** The physical and/or psychological dependence on alcohol or other mood-altering drugs or chemicals that is marked by frequent and heavy use, growing tolerance, inability to abstain without discomfort, continued use despite consequences, and, in many cases, physical withdrawal. The term addiction is often applied to other compulsive disorders such as gambling, overeating, and sexual disorders because the dynamics of obsession, compulsion, loss of control, adverse consequences, and denial are so similar.

**Affective Therapy:** A form of therapy that teaches people how to recognize, label, and tell other people about their feelings and emotions. Affective therapy involves the use of mental imagery and experiential therapy techniques that help people to experience their feelings and emotions more fully and express them both verbally and nonverbally. The goal is to teach people how to manage their feelings and emotions without having to use alcohol, drugs, or criminal behaviors.

**Alcoholics Anonymous (AA):** An organization of recovering alcoholics who work to help themselves and others recover from alcoholism. AA is based on twelve recommended steps to recovery that form the basis of many related Twelve Step programs such as Narcotics Anonymous (NA) and Cocaine Anonymous (CA).

**Antisocial Behaviors:** Any action that defies established laws, morality, or sense of justice and fair play. Antisocial behaviors can be conscious and volitional or they can be unconscious or accidental.

**Awfulizing Sobriety:** A form of irrational thinking used by chemically dependent criminal offenders to convince themselves that it is better to go back to the use of alcohol, drugs, and criminal behavior than it is to stay sober. When people "awfulize sobriety," they tell themselves that maintaining abstinence from alcohol, drugs, and criminal behaviors is awful or terrible. They tell themselves that the consequences of being abstinent are far worse than the consequences of using alcohol, drugs, and criminal behaviors.

**Basic Beliefs:** Ideas that people have about themselves, other people, and the world. These beliefs may be accurate in that they correspond to objective external reality, or they may be mistaken in that the person believes they are true even though there is no evidence to support them. A primary goal in the treatment of chemically dependent criminal offenders is to help them identify and challenge the mistaken beliefs that lead them back to the use of alcohol, drugs, and criminal behaviors.

**Behavioral Therapy:** A form of therapy that teaches people how to identify self-defeating behaviors and replace them with constructive behaviors. Behavioral therapy involves the use of role playing, behavioral instruction, behavior change assignments, behavioral rehearsal, and practice techniques.

**Biopsychosocial Model:** A model of recovery that promotes the identification and resolution of the biological (physical), psychological (mental and emotional), and social (relationship and situation) problems that have been caused by chemical dependency and criminal personality traits which will lead to relapse if they are not dealt with.

**Chemical Dependency:** The psychological and social dependence on or the addiction to alcohol and other mood-altering drugs. The term chemical dependency is used to describe what DSM IIIR calls "Substance Use Disorders." There are two types of substance use disorders. An *abuse disorder* occurs when a person has psychological and social problems resulting from alcohol and drug use but is not physically addicted. A *dependence disorder* occurs when a person is physically addicted (see definition of addiction).

**Cognitive Therapy:** A form of therapy that is directed at teaching people to identify irrational thinking, challenge irrational thoughts as they arise in day-to-day living, and replace irrational thoughts with rational and more helpful ways of thinking.

**Compulsion:** A strong or overwhelming emotional urge to do something. Compulsion often has a target such as the use of alcohol, drugs, or criminal behavior. Compulsions to use are often accompanied by obsession (the out-of-control thinking about use) and craving (the physical tissue hunger for the drug).

**Core Addictive Issues:** Problems that result directly from the abuse or addictive use of alcohol or drugs that must be resolved in sobriety. Typical core addictive issues include intoxication; withdrawal; alcohol- and drug-centered living; denial; or work, social, or intimate problems caused by the addiction.

**Core Criminal Issues:** Problems that result directly from the use of criminal thinking and criminal behavior that must be resolved in sobriety. Typical core criminal issues include the compulsive need to break rules and challenge authority, the need to be the constant center of attention, the need to view other people as objects who deserve to be used and manipulated, impulse control problems that result in disruptive acting-out behaviors, and the desire to constantly con, cheat, and hustle others.

**Core Psychological Issues:** Problems that result directly from mistaken beliefs that were formed in childhood and continue to be held as adults even though they are no longer true. These beliefs focus on the self (Who am I as a person and what am I about in my life?), other people (Who others are as people and what are they about in their lives?), and the world in general (What kind of place is this to live and what have I a right to expect from my environment?). These mistaken beliefs cause people to act out with self-defeating behaviors.

**Counseling:** The process of helping a person to: (1) identify and clarify specific problems; (2) identify the patterns of thinking, feeling, and acting that cause or complicate the problems; (3) use systematic problem-solving methods in resolving the problems; and (4) provide support and encouragement during the problem-resolution process.

**Craving:** A powerful physical desire that demands satisfaction. When used in relation to alcohol or drugs, it refers to the physical need for the drug to normalize brain chemistry or to medicate the symptoms of alcohol or drug withdrawal.

**Dependency:** The reliance on the use of alcohol or other mood-altering drugs to comfortably complete one or more life tasks. The severity of dependency can be measured by (1) how many tasks have become dependent on alcohol and drugs for successful completion, and (2) how difficult it is to complete a task without alcohol and drug use.

**Detoxification:** A procedure that is designed to help people recover from the symptoms of withdrawal immediately after they stop using alcohol and other drugs. There are two types of detoxification: *medical detoxification* for people suffering from severe alcohol and drug withdrawal, and *nonmedical detoxification* for people with mild withdrawal symptoms. Medical detoxification involves using medication in gradually lower and lower doses until the person is totally drug free and has no withdrawal symptoms. Nonmedical detoxification involves using behavioral and social supports to help a person manage the withdrawal symptoms. *Behavioral/medical detoxification* involves the use of both medical and nonmedical approaches in combination.

**Developmental Model of Recovery:** A way of thinking about recovery as a process that occurs in steps and stages. The CENAPS Developmental Model of Recovery divides the recovery process into six stages: *transition*, during which people recognize they have a disease or disorder and become willing to recover; *stabilization*, during which people heal physically and psychologically and resolve the immediate crisis caused by their disease or disorder; *early recovery*, during which people learn to identify and change the irrational thoughts that developed to protect them from confronting the reality of their disease or disorder; *middle recovery*, during which people repair lifestyle damage caused by the disease or disorder and develop a balanced, healthy lifestyle; *late recovery*, during which people make deep changes in personality and values necessary to lower chronic life stress and minimize long-term risk of relapse; and *maintenance*, during which people continue to grow and develop and guard against relapse.

**Dysfunctional:** Being unable to act or behave in a normal manner, to successfully complete normal acts of daily living, or to accomplish realistic life goals.

**Euphoric Recall:** A pattern of irrational thinking in which a person remembers and exaggerates the good times associated with the use of alcohol, drugs, or criminal behavior

219

while minimizing or blocking out any bad or negative memories.

**Feelings:** (1) An emotion, such as anger, sadness, joy, sorrow, or frustration; (2) A body sensation, such as hunger, tenseness, being cold, a stiff neck, or other physical reactions.

**Habit:** Something that we do automatically and without thinking.

**Injunctions:** An irrational thought that mistakenly tells people that they cannot, should not, or must not do something. Each injunction carries the implied threat of a negative consequence if it is not obeyed. The negative consequence can be mild ("I will feel ashamed or guilty"), moderate ("Something awful or terrible will happen to me"), or severe ("I will die"). (Also see *Mandates*.)

**Irrational Thoughts:** Thoughts that don't correspond with objective and verifiable external reality.

**Loss of Control:** The inability to predict what will happen once alcohol and drug use begins or the inability to abstain despite conscious commitments to do so. People can lose control over what happens while using alcohol and drugs, over their ability to stop once they have begun to use, or over their ability to refrain from use. They can also lose control of their behavior while abstinent as a result of severe stress, obsession, compulsion, or craving.

**Magical Thinking:** The general belief that something can be accomplished without completing the steps necessary to accomplish it. When applied to the use of alcohol, drugs, and criminal behavior, it refers to the belief that the use of these things will fix the user or solve problems without having to do anything else.

**Mandates:** An irrational thought that mistakenly tells people they must, should, or have to do something. Each mandate carries the implied threat of negative consequences if it is not obeyed. The negative consequence can be mild ("I will feel ashamed or guilty"), moderate ("Something awful or terrible will happen to me"), or severe ("I will die"). (Also see *Injunction*.)

**Mistaken Belief:** An incorrect belief learned in childhood or as a result of adult experiences that is thought to be true even though it is not true. Mistaken beliefs form the truth as a person believes it to be. As a result, when people act on mistaken beliefs they often develop problems and cannot identify their role in creating the problem.

**Narcotics Anonymous (NA):** An organization of recovering drug addicts who work together to help themselves and others recover from addiction by using the Twelve Steps.

**Obsession:** Out-of-control thinking that is intrusive, rigid, and repetitive. Chemically dependent criminal offenders are often obsessed by thoughts of using alcohol, drugs, and criminal behaviors.

**Personality:** A set of enduring and deeply entrenched habits of perceiving, thinking, feeling, acting, and relating to self, others, and the world. Personality is developed in early childhood and unconsciously acted out in adulthood unless conscious efforts are made to identify and change the habitual patterns associated with the childhood personality style.

**Personality Disorder:** Extremely self-defeating personality styles that are marked by the repetitive use of irrational thinking and self-defeating behavior that results in the development of physical, psychological, and social problems that prevent normal functioning in one or more areas. The person with a personality disorder will defend and maintain the self-defeating style despite the serious problems and consequences.

**Psychotherapy:** A specific treatment designed to change personality disorders that consist of teaching people how to identify and change their rigid patterns of self-defeating

221

thinking, feeling management, and behaviors. This is done by teaching clients about the personality disorders they have, showing them why their personality is not working for them, and teaching them about healthy personality traits. Clients are then guided in a self-evaluation of their own personality style and asked to decide if it is healthy or self-defeating. Clients are asked to make a commitment to change by identifying and modifying the specific self-defeating patterns of perceiving, thinking, feeling, acting, and relating that are causing problems. Strategies for changing these habitual ways of being need to be developed, and long-term support and reinforcement for new, more effective ways of being must be provided.

**Recovery:** A developmental process of moving from experiencing the symptoms of a disease or disorder through various stages in which the symptoms became less severe and eventually go away altogether. (See also *Developmental Model of Recovery*.)

**Relapse:** The return of the symptoms of a disease or disorder after it has been treated successfully and brought into remission. The CENAPS Model views relapse as a process of reactivating the symptoms of a disease or disorder. In this model there are observable warning signs that precede the reactivation of severe symptoms. These warning signs can be identified and managed early before the disease or disorder is reactivated.

**Relapse Syndrome:** A specific collection of progressive symptoms or relapse warning signs that leads a person from stable recovery back into alcohol and drug use. In this context, relapse can be defined as the process of becoming so dysfunctional in recovery that a person returns to alcohol and drug use in an attempt to cope with or manage the dysfunction.

**Relapse Justification:** An irrational thought that recovering people tell themselves that convinces them it is OK to return to the use of alcohol, drugs, or criminal behaviors after they have started a recovery program.

**Recreational Drug Users:** The use of mood-altering drugs for enjoyment by people who do not experience any noticeable physical, psychological, or social dependence or problems.

**Relapse Prevention Therapy (RPT):** A specialty treatment process designed to help people with a chronic disease or disorder to identify and intervene on the early warning signs that can cause relapse. The CENAPS Model of Relapse Prevention has four components: assessment, warning sign identification, warning sign management, and recovery planning.

**Relapse Warning Signs:** A series of thoughts, feelings, and actions triggered by a situation or condition that leads from stable recovery to alcohol or drug use.

**Self-defeating Behavior:** Actions that people take to solve a problem or create a positive consequence that end up making the problem worse or creating a negative consequence. Many self-defeating behaviors are deeply entrenched, automatic, and unconscious habits.

**Social Drinkers:** People who consume alcoholic beverages without experiencing any noticeable physical, psychological, or social problems and never have any serious problems as a result of their use.

**Tolerance:** The ability to consume large quantities of alcohol or other mood-altering drugs without feeling or appearing to be intoxicated.

**Unmanageable Feeling:** Feelings people do not want to have or pretend they don't have until they react in a negative way.

**Thought:** The personally perceived outcome of thinking. Thinking is the mental process of perceiving, assigning words and symbols to what is perceived, and manipulating those symbols with the goal of understanding or making sense out what is perceived.